Praise for *Words That Work*

Cindy McGill is a passionate lover of people—ALL people. For the many years I have walked closely with her, I have always been impressed with her genuine zeal for reaching those trapped in deceptive darkness. She has for years effectively taught the Body of Christ how to authentically love and reach the lost. She is also one of the most creative ministers I know as she effectively clothes truth in ways that those not churched will understand.

This book will open your eyes to many fresh and insightful concepts and tools. You might even identify some religious habits and patterns in yourself as you learn how to communicate the Good News in more effective ways.

Patricia King
Founder, Patricia King Ministries

This is one of the most important books I know of for anyone who has a heart for revival and awakening. God has given Cindy McGill a unique ability to reach those that other people would not even try to reach. It is eye-opening, challenging, and an absolute must for believers everywhere to read.

Cindy Jacobs
Generals International

Cindy McGill was born as a prophetic evangelist to bring God's healing light into the darkest places, where hearts are confused, offended, and hurting, yet still seeking for real truth and godly answers, just in the wrong places. In her latest book, *Words That Work*, Cindy gives the necessary nuts and bolts to approaching the unbeliever with words of wisdom straight from the Father's heart of love.

The apostle Paul said, "I become all things to all men that I may win some to Christ Jesus." Cindy skillfully demonstrates a higher way of evangelizing a lost world. Through the written words she chooses, Cindy paints a simple, practical picture that demonstrates what actions to take to instill hope and which ones to avoid in order to be a successful soul winner. By learning to adopt, follow, and apply this updated ministry blueprint designed for this current era, you will introduce many people to Christ.

Dr. Barbie L. Breathitt
Best-selling author of the *A to Z Dream Symbology Dictionary* and 20 additional books
DreamsDecoder.com, DecodeMyDream.com,
BarbieBreathitt.com

When we first met Cindy McGill, we were both blown away by her simple yet effective outreach methods. We couldn't believe that in our forty-plus years of ministry, we had never heard anyone else talk about reaching the lost the way Cindy did. Not only that, but she was going into the dark places where most Christians wouldn't step foot. She is fearless in her love for the lost and is especially effective in reaching those who are searching for life's meaning in all the wrong places. She knows how to reach those that seem unreachable, those who are looking for spiritual connection, and those who are completely lost and broken.

Cindy has worked hard over the years to put language to her ministry and outreach that helps to break down walls and open hearts. Now you have the opportunity to learn from Cindy's vast experience and tried and true methods in her new book *Words That Work*. You, too, can learn to minister to the lost in power. You will be able to ditch the Christianese language that puts non-believers on the defensive, and have greater conversation because you're relatable, rather than putting them on the defensive because they're not familiar with your language. You will find it's easier to connect, have meaningful conversations, and win the lost when you reach out with words that work!

Craig & Suzy Nelson
Miracles in the Marketplace International

Cindy's got the formula and you need this book. More than any human being I know, God's downloaded the how-to-do-it model for taking Jesus to the streets. Please get this book and also get one for a friend while you're at it. It's that good!

Cindy McGill is one of those women of God who is on my heroes list. She willingly and regularly goes into the dark places on Earth and ministers to those greatly affected or caught by the enemy himself. She has made it her cause to rescue the perishing!

Steve Shultz
Founder, THE ELIJAH LIST

The first time I heard Cindy McGill share how she was able to effectively bring the gospel to hearts that seem so dark and unreachable, I was undone. I became adamant that she share at our women's conference and any other space I could get her to equip us. She holds a key that God chose to give her, which can access the heart of a person in the darkest of places! I want that! I want that for the church! I want that for all of us. This book is that key!

If we will become a humble student, letting go of our religious patterns, we will win the world to Christ. And the best part … we will see these precious people know our amazing King. I'm so happy to have this book to recommend to everyone I know.

Jenny Donnelly
Founder of Tetelestai Ministries & Her Voice Movement
Co-Founder of the Collective Church in Portland Oregon

WORDS
THAT
WORK

WORDS THAT WORK

A LANGUAGE
OF LIGHT
for A
WORLD
LIVING IN
DARKNESS

CINDY McGILL

WORDS THAT WORK

Copyright © 2021 Cindy McGill

Published by Hope for the Harvest
CindyMcGill.org
Dallas, Texas USA

No part of this book may be reproduced, stored in a retrieval system or transmitted in any form or by any means—electronic, mechanical, photocopy, recording or any other—except for brief quotations, without permission in writing from the author.

No part of this book may be reproduced, stored in a retrieval system or transmitted in any form or by any means—electronic, mechanical, photocopy, recording or any other—except for brief quotations, without permission in writing from the author.

Unless otherwise noted, all Scripture quotations are taken from the New King James Version® Copyright © 1982 by Thomas Nelson. Used by permission. All rights reserved. Scripture marked HCSB is from the Holman Christian Standard Bible, copyright © 1999, 2000, 2002, 2003, 2009 by Holman Bible Publishers, Nashville Tennessee. All rights reserved. Scripture marked KJV is from the King James Bible, which is in the public domain. Scripture marked NCV is from The Holy Bible, New Century Version®. Copyright © 2005 by Thomas Nelson, Inc. Scripture marked RSV is from the Revised Standard Version of the Bible, copyright © 1946, 1952, and 1971 the Division of Christian Education of the National Council of the Churches of Christ in the United States of America. Used by permission. All rights reserved.

Edited by Elizabeth H. Sluka
Typesetting by Katherine Lloyd at theDESKonline.com
Cover by Tommy Owen at TommyOwenDesign.com

Printed in the United States of America

21 22 23 24 25   5 4 3 2 1

TABLE OF CONTENTS

Foreword xi
Introduction... 1
1 Why We Must Change Our Language.................... 9
2 Finding Highways and Hedges 17
3 Three Primary Groups of Culture..................... 27
4 The Counterculture/Cancel Culture Dilemma 35
5 The Power of Dreams 41
6 Using Words That Work at Outreach Events 51
7 New Language to Reach the Seekers................... 61
8 There's No Hurt Like Church Hurt.................... 81
9 The Heart of the Seeker Generation 85
10 God's Heart for the Seekers 105
11 It's Fun to Build Bridges........................... 123
12 They Will Know Us by Our Love....................... 143
   Appendix: Say This and Not That..................... 149
   About the Author 157

FOREWORD

Words That Work is a title that really grabs me. Any time any person sits down to write and finish a book, the title is a really big deal. Every Christian and follower of Jesus would do well to study the titles given to Jesus throughout the Bible. Some of the notably great titles out of the 134 biblically listed are God, Savior, Lord, Prophet, Priest, and King. "The One," found in the book of Revelation, is one of my favorites, but here is a revelatory title most of the church would never be compatible with: "Friend of Sinners."

You may never have heard that biblical title before, but Jesus is actually called the Friend of Sinners. It wasn't given to Him by those who celebrated Him, but it should have been. Apparently, his enemies branded Him as such, and Jesus repeated it to indicate their view of Him in Matthew 11:18-19:

> "For John came neither eating nor drinking, and they say, 'He has a demon.' The Son of Man came eating and drinking, and they say, 'Look, a glutton and a

winebibber, a friend of tax collectors and sinners!' But wisdom is justified by her children."

"John was separate from everything cultural," they said, "so it's proof he has a devil." Jesus was actively pursuing people in all aspects of culture, so they accused him of unholy filth and called Him demonically carnal. While He denied their accusation of unholiness, He repeated the title of Friend of Sinners. I think He liked it and it became adopted into the church's understanding of His mercy and determination to actually reach the lost.

Now, this title of King Jesus also really grabs me. Sadly, the majority of us in the church have been known for who we stand against rather than those we stand for. I know Jesus is hoping we will change that.

Cindy McGill has spent decades of her life taking the gospel of Jesus into the mission fields of New Age, witchcraft, pornography, and even paranormal spiritualism. Her fearless determination to actually see people saved and set free has come from her conviction that Jesus actually loves these people many church folk dismiss as unredeemable.

You should see her in action. I have been with her in several public places, and how she gets to the heart of the person in front of her is prophetic and relational.

She can teach us something.

Through the years, she has searched long and hard for words that work in parts of the world that do not speak "Christianese," the language of the American church. Like

FOREWORD

a loving mama, she has patiently found ways to effectively communicate deep spiritual truth and the love of Jesus, and demonstrate Him in genuine ways to the lost.

When she first started, the crazy people she engaged with were considered the lunatic fringe. That extreme darkness has now become mainstream culture, and the Lord has positioned Cindy to be ahead of the curve.

The body of Christ needs a serious change in its understanding of the cause of Jesus toward the unbeliever. We also need to own the effectiveness of our impact. It means we have to be willing to readjust our methods and completely change our wineskins. This book is a compilation of Cindy's simple solutions in the complicated issues of how to actually communicate the heart of Jesus.

We should judge a book not by the content or even the way it is written, but by the impact it makes on us. How do you judge *The Diary of Anne Frank* or *Aesop's Fables*? You determine the worth of those writings by the impact, or the fruit, you might say. Matthew 7:20 says, "Therefore, by their fruits you will know them."

You also consider the fruit of those books in context to the field or the day and society they were written and delivered in. Impact is the consequence, not of method but of effectiveness. The methods are not the goal. Effectiveness is the goal, and impact is the consequence. Just like that, we should truly measure our evangelism not by the method or tradition but by the reality of the impact we are actually making.

In the Kingdom, what is real really matters. In the

Kingdom, the impact you make is a much higher priority for the warrior bride than the feeling of accomplishment that comes from the attempt. Real transformational impact is a big deal if you are actually trying to advance the Kingdom.

Sadly, our fight for traditional methods has caused us to fight for things that no longer matter. The consequence is a lost generation that doesn't understand our language or our priorities.

The Spirit of God is giving true Kingdom people a passionate heart to reach the lost in previously taboo places in society. Our own culture is hungry for truth and desperately needs a missionary willing to learn their language in order to reach them.

What's real is what matters, and the Bible calls that term "truth." Truth is not your ability to speak King James. Truth is the person of King Jesus. As ambassadors of Truth, we lean hard into being ministers of reconciliation in order that we have to learn the power of words that work.

A few years back, I had a dream and a true visitation from God. I was in a dark place with no colors. Everything was in black and white. Walking through something like a hall, I entered into a room and found a big ball of yarn wadded up on the floor. I reached down, picked it up, and saw that it was knotted and tangled with all sizes of different-colored strings that stood out in the black and white scene. It wasn't pretty. To me, it looked something like a rat's nest, and I immediately got frustrated with the mess of it.

I really wanted to unwind it, but it was obviously an impossible puzzle to solve. I felt a dread about the task of making

FOREWORD

it straight. The more I looked at it, the more anxiety I felt. I decided to pull out a lighter, set it on fire, and watch the whole thing burn.

Just as I was about to give up, I noticed a small, tiny thread rising from the mess and I knew it was the answer to unwinding the whole thing. I pinched it between my finger and thumb, held the weight of the ball, and yanked hard. Suddenly the ball began to spin and thread down to my feet. It rolled completely across the room and unwound from my hand into a perfectly straight line of string.

As soon as it was completely unwound, I heard a voice—an angel carrying a prophetic declaration, I believe. "Simple solutions to complicated issues!" he declared.

I am praying this book will be a catalyst for a personal revival. I hope you see the wadded-up issues of evangelism come completely untangled with simple verbal solutions.

Cindy has a ministry to the lost that works wonders. True jaw-dropping wonders. Her ministry has worked through the decades like a fearless demonstration of freedom, redemption, and the goodness of God. I am so happy she is sharing her heart and her mind, and I'm so proud of her for sharing her Words That Work.

I am challenged and excited, and you should be too.

—**Troy Brewer**
Senior Pastor of OpenDoor Church in Burleson, Texas,
and author of *Redeeming Your Timeline, Numbers that Preach, Good Overcomes Evil, Looking Up* and *Soul Invasion*
TroyBrewer.com

I will not stay inside the church,
I will not stay upon my perch.
I will go out into this land,
I will be led by His own hand.
I'll see with eyes from heaven's side
and move within the darkest tide.
I'll reach into the hearts of man
and obey the voice of His command.
The ones who thought they'd never come
will see His LIGHT and to Him they'll run.
They feel the Spirit of the Truth
that lifts them up beyond the roof.
When He gets inside their heart,
they understand their brand-new start.
No matter what they've said or done,
their eyes are open, they speak in tongues.
Even though they've barely met,
they do not want to leave just yet.
I feel Him looking through my eyes,
that shatters all the devil's lies.
They say they did not think it so,
but He knows just where to go.
Removing dirt and words that sting,
He replaces them with songs to sing.
A cleansing flood, He pours it down

and causes them to hit the ground.
He's rescuing the ones He loves
with power flowing from above.
They ask us "Can I have this now?"
and THEN we tell them WHO and HOW.
We say, "His name is Jesus Christ,
the son of God who gave His life."
They weep and cry as freedom comes
and surrender hearts to the ONLY ONE.
This is how we see it done
as God receives another one.
The devil's plan is foiled again
as we move on to move with Him!

By Cindy McGill
A tribute to Burning Man
and all the ground we take for Him.

INTRODUCTION

God is for us. He has much for us to do as we are approaching the biggest spiritual awakening this earth has ever seen. Obstacles and tough situations we may experience are nothing for God to create smooth pathways from twisted and crooked ones. He is with us, in us, moving through us, and is more than able to protect and deliver us from anything that may try and hinder or sabotage our lives.

Over the years, I have watched God give us the most amazing instructions and blueprints for outreach efforts we have done. Our teams have found ourselves going into places where the church is definitely not present. Such places are "feeding frenzies" for people who have no identity, no truth on the inside of them, no direction, and "church hurt" issues. As a result, they have embraced alternative lifestyles that are contrary to the original design God intended His people to live in.

All throughout the Bible, we read story after story of champions who lived in very difficult times, yet overcame the circumstances of those days by following God's instructions for that moment and battle. Every battle has a victorious strategy and every difficulty offers us a way to learn how God will deliver us when we take His direction and not lean on our own understanding.

In this book, I am offering you some of the strategic pathways God instructed us to take and language He asked us to use to fulfill our purpose in reaching cultures where people are far from God and hardened toward spiritual things in general. Present-day "life" is filled with darkness and confusion. God sends us into this world as His carriers of light. As we see the day of Jesus drawing near, the cultural extremes are intensifying.

People are in full-blown rebellion, living lives built on lies and emotions, and are in need of a solid foundation which can only be found on the Rock, Christ Jesus. God instructed us to use a "stealthier" approach in navigating this world. My hope is that you will read this book with an open mind and a teachable heart, understanding the times and seasons we are currently living in and how God is training us in His ways and how to think His thoughts. Isaiah 55:8 says, "For My thoughts are not your thoughts, nor are your ways My ways, says the Lord."

Let's look at Matthew 10:16–22:

> "Behold, I send you out as sheep in the midst of wolves. Therefore be wise as serpents and harmless as doves. But beware of men, for they will deliver you up to councils and scourge you in their synagogues.

INTRODUCTION

You will be brought before governors and kings for My sake, as a testimony to them and to the Gentiles. But when they deliver you up, do not worry about how or what you should speak. For it will be given to you in that hour what you should speak; for it is not you who speak, but the Spirit of your Father who speaks in you."

As lawlessness increases, it's accompanied by a spirit of offense. Proverbs 18:19 says, "A brother offended is harder to win than a strong city, and contentions are like the bars of a castle."

Offense is a tool of hell to keep people divided and fighting. If the devil can keep people fighting, separated by petty differences and harboring grudges with each other about anything, then unity will not be available for people, families, and our world to heal. In Mark 13:12-13, Jesus says, "Now brother will betray brother to death, and a father his child; and children will rise up against parents and cause them to be put to death. And you will be hated by all for My name's sake. But he who endures to the end shall be saved."

Jesus told us what to expect in the last days. This book will help you understand the current culture, mindset, time, and season we are living in and give you language, strategy, and boldness to engage this harvest that is awakening and hungering for God.

(In Alan Hirsch's book *The Forgotten Ways*, he communicated the idea that most contemporary church models are effective to reach 40 percent of our culture. My intention in writing this book is to present a process that has proven effective in reaching the other 60 percent that will statistically not respond to present-day contemporary church models.)

We are being fashioned by God and He is creating a new wine skin in us to hold new wine for these days, as you will read about in this book.

WE ARE BEING CENSORED AND BLAMED

This book is about uncharted territory, navigating the world we currently we live in, and the strange and beautiful people who inhabit it. It's about a God whose love is so radical and so complete that He is desperate for us to blaze trails into the hearts of the ones who occupy the outer limits. While it looks like they could not be farther from Him, it turns out they are closer than they, or we, could have ever guessed.

You may know some of these people in these alternative lifestyles. They may be in your family. They may be friends, neighbors, or acquaintances. If you don't have a clue how to reach them, there is hope. I've hacked out a path for you, so read on.

I feel it is of absolute importance that we learn how to become wise and "stealthy" in navigating spiritual land mines through troubled times as more and more spiritual freedoms are removed from us, our culture, our churches, our nation, and the world abroad. We are in a spiritual battle unlike any we've been in before. Underground churches all over the world have been using an approach, just like the one I am

INTRODUCTION

presenting, for years—especially in places and times of persecution. In this book, I will uncover the tip of the iceberg, so to speak, of new approaches and language, as well as some helpful instructions. These proven strategies will enable you to go the distance in speaking truth to a world who desperately needs to hear it but has become walled up to the typical approaches of the Christian church.

Please understand that this will be written in specific language and phraseology to help us navigate the days ahead safely, powerfully, and unapologetically. By using this, we can navigate such groups unashamed of the "Power" and the "Life" who lives in us and flows through us. We are being retrained in new ways of communication that will set a table for the Bread of Life to be served to spiritually hungry and confused people the world over. If applied, the contents of this book, these "words that work," will benefit you immensely in your relationships and outreach efforts.

The church's approach to reaching others is horribly outdated and in need of refining. Speaking truth in simple words and parabolic language will enable us to advance the message of Jesus to a world who has been convinced that they are condemned by Him rather than loved by Him—if they even believe He exists at all. Just take a look at how Jesus spoke to the multitudes. He spoke to them in parables.

According to Mark 4:34, "But without a parable He did not speak to them." We will be touching on the power of dreams and their interpretation, which are always parabolic because God said in Joel 2:28 that dreams would be poured out "on all flesh." This means that people who do and do not know Him will be receiving God messages through their dreams.

Jesus calls Himself "the Way, the Truth, and the Life" instead of calling Himself Jesus, as we learn when Jesus asks Peter in Matthew 16:13, "Who do men say that I, the Son of Man, am?" Though some may not understand, and some may even disagree, I can assure you this language is easy to understand and communicate for people who live in deep darkness.

I can assure you that these strategies work and will keep you from getting yourself into arguments and precarious situations in the future. I have spoken to people who are assigned as missionaries to the Middle East, China, and so many other places around the world, where these methods are absolutely essential in maintaining not only their missionary efforts, but also protecting their lives. I have created outreach teams since the late 1990s, not only to bring God's power into counterculture arenas, but also into extreme, spiritually contested areas where people are most certainly not God-friendly and have hate toward those who carry the message of the one Messiah named Jesus.

I have lots of history I could share with you about our spiritual journeys and pastoral experience, but briefly, I'll just say that my husband and I have pastored four interdenominational churches over a span of forty years and have a great respect and honor for the "Spirit of Truth," as well as His expressions and revivals over the years. We all have our own spiritual journey. If there must be a label, we define ourselves as "followers of Jesus." This statement represents a

INTRODUCTION

personal spiritual path, word of testimony, and the "blood of the Lamb," which we refer to as the "red purifying life flow" that powerfully overcomes darkness and Satan according to Revelation 12:11.

We have pioneered churches in hard places, many in Utah, so we are skilled in defusing arguments from people who are bound by a spirit of religion. The religious love to argue and throw Scriptures out as if they were fly fishing—hoping you'll bite. This book will address the how-tos of avoiding these kinds of rabbit-hole traps.

When the Spirit is moving in power and the atmosphere is shifting and changing, there is much more freedom to say what is needed. However, these are proven words and phrases that will defuse and deflect potential arguments in most spiritual climates.

Having met God during the "Jesus Movement" of the 1970s, I have watched the church struggle with effective ways to communicate God's love to a dying world outside its often-closed doors. The lost and lonely wanderers among us desperately need to know Jesus loves them. He is compelling them back into their original purpose, which is better than anything man can offer.

CHAPTER 1

WHY WE MUST CHANGE OUR LANGUAGE

We live in a world that has largely rejected Christ and everything to do with Him. Just compare any school, workplace, or store today with the ones that existed only eighty years ago. The geography is the same, but the culture has changed. Approaching people with "Christianese" nowadays is like trying to speak English to a Frenchman. Not only will people not understand what you're trying to say, but they may get angry because your words sound rude in their ears.

At the same time, people are desperately seeking purpose and meaning. God wants to encounter them where they are, which means that we need to learn their language in order to communicate the love of God their souls desperately crave. Followers of Jesus need to be stealthy and strategic cultural ambassadors so that seekers can openly accept the gift of grace.

It's actually very dangerous and hurtful when people go "Christianese" crazy in places where we must be stealthy. My friend spent two full years building a bridge of trust going into the brothels in Nevada. Dennis Hof was the owner. You might remember him as the man who ran and won a Republican seat in Nevada for state representative after he was dead. He owned the Moonlite Bunny Ranch in the middle of the Nevada desert.

My friend would take gifts to the girls in the brothel and just bless them. She never used religious words or language that would create barriers or prevent her team from being able to minister and encourage the girls. Her entire team was on the same page with these strategies. One year, however, a team member took it upon herself to share Jesus out loud with the girls, telling them about hell and how much their lifestyles had disappointed God. My friend got that woman out of there as soon as she realized what was happening, but a week later she received a letter from Dennis Hof.

> This is Dennis Hof. I just spent an hour listening to our girls tell us how you made them cry and scared them with your religion and wanting to save them. Because of this, we are not allowing any church ladies in our locations in southern or northern Nevada or strip club. Please do not attempt to come into our businesses. God doesn't want you hurting people, and

the manager of the brothels has told me, "Ban them all, Dennis, protect the girls." This is not open for discussion.

My friend's *entire* outreach was discontinued as a result of one person being reckless and not following the guidelines on this effort. People in that industry and other places have to be reached the way God knows they do. Our responsibility is to follow Jesus, not take matters into our own hands and go off on a religious rant or use old methods of evangelism.

The last two years that we went to the porn convention, we noticed that the Christian booths that had paid to go into the event and give away New Testament Bibles, prayer boards, and books from Christian authors were *not* allowed back into the convention, no matter how much they would pay for a booth. Because we sign up our teams as "dream interpreters," we were given badges each year without question and were able to continue our outreach efforts.

There is a reason Jesus told people to be *wise* as serpents and harmless as doves in Matthew 10:16. God has a plan and strategy for every outreach, and if we don't follow His lead, we will not be allowed into certain places. It only takes one person who decides to follow their own will and emotions—jumping ahead, getting religious, and saying things God isn't asking us to say at that moment—to completely disqualify outreach efforts by other followers of Jesus.

Jesus doesn't want any to perish, and He wants us to use our words and language to reach people most effectively. Let's turn to look at the groups of seekers Jesus lays out in the New Testament.

FOUR GROUPS OF SEEKERS

In the book of Luke, we read the parable of the Great Supper, where a table was prepared by a very generous man. Invitations to the amazing feast were sent, we can assume, to friends and family—people who were personally known to the man, which explains the invitation. Luke 14:18–24 says:

> But they all with one accord began to make excuses. The first said to him, "I have bought a piece of ground, and I must go and see it. I ask you to have me excused."
>
> And another said, "I have bought five yoke of oxen, and I am going to test them. I ask you to have me excused." Still another said, "I have married a wife, and therefore I cannot come." So that servant came and reported these things to his master.
>
> Then the master of the house, being angry, said to his servant, "Go out quickly into the streets and lanes of the city, and bring in here the poor and the maimed and the lame and the blind."
>
> And the servant said, "Master, it is done as you commanded, and still there is room."
>
> Then the master said to the servant, "Go out into the highways and hedges, and compel them to come in, that my house may be filled. For I say to you that none of those men who were invited shall taste my supper."

Business and finances, achievements, friends and family—the cares of this life were more important than their relationship with the generous man. Does this sound familiar?

Let's look at this prophetic parable from heaven's perspective.

Jesus lays out four distinct categories of life: the poor, the maimed, the lame, and the blind. Each category has a distinct compelling factor, which tells us that not all methods work on all people. Jesus told us to follow Him and He would actually make us fishers of men. So, just who does He want us to fish for and how do we catch them?

THE POOR

First, Jesus pointed out the poor. These, He said in Matthew 26:11, "you will always have with you." The poor come with a promise: if we give to the poor, we're really lending to the Lord and He will repay us for what we have given (see Proverbs 19:17). Feeding and helping the poor is a great outreach opportunity for those just getting their feet wet in reaching seekers, and the reward is immediate.

THE LAME

Next, Jesus mentions the lame. I've found these to be people with spiritual legs but without strength or direction. Cut off from their identity, they have legs, but there is no strength in their spiritual walk. These are the creatives who don't think like everyone else—artisans, dancers, musicians, poets, and philosophers. They seem more in touch with their "spirit" than with reality, but are they? These people are cut off at the knees by an alternate identity and warped perception of love. They think they know who they are and where they are going, but they're really limping along in the wrong direction. God knows who they were created to be, but I've discovered they don't have a clue.

THE MAIMED

The maimed are compelled to the "feast" by their need for stable relationships. They crave people who can go the distance with them and not bail. Because of their brokenness, their true Kingdom worth is unrecognizable. They don't know who you are because they don't know who they are. Marked by abandonment and rejection, the maimed do not trust because their relationships are blown up by abuse and deception. They've been used, devalued, despised, and lied to. Hurt and afraid, they hide or lash out. How do you reach the maimed? On an installment plan: a little down and a little each month. Rebuilding trust bridges isn't easy. With the maimed, you have to be in it for the long haul—no falling out, no losing focus, no dropping the ball.

THE BLIND

Finally, the blind are brought to the table. These people bump into the same walls and stumble over the same obstacles again and again. Wandering aimlessly through life, they are visionless and generally happen upon a cliff. The King James Bible puts it in these brutal terms:

> Where there is no vision, the people perish: but he that keepeth the law, happy is he. (Proverbs 29:18 KJV)

While vision can be an ability to see the big picture, it also has some other interesting meanings. The lack of it has some interesting manifestations, as seen in alternate translations of this passage:

> Where there is no prophecy the people cast off restraint. (RSV)
>
> Where there is no word from God, people are uncontrolled. (NCV)
>
> Without revelation people run wild. (HCSB)

A lack of vision, or being able to see and understand, leads to chaos. Dreams die. Identity, purpose, and destiny wither away. Not being able to see, hear, or understand God, the sightless cannot connect to Him. They need Jesus to be revealed to them to have the life they are looking for. So, who are the blind in practical terms?

They are the seekers of New Age, the mystics of witchcraft, and the sojourners of Eastern religions that have no power. They long for power and purpose, but their mistake is attempting to get it apart from relationship with the Holy Spirit. Their hearts are open to hear and receive because their lack of direction has developed an insatiable hunger to find life, purpose, and direction. They are actually closer to God than you think.

CHAPTER 2

FINDING HIGHWAYS AND HEDGES

From Jesus' parable of the Great Supper in Luke 14, we see that the host of the feast told his servants to immediately go out and *compel* them to come in. Go out *now* into the highways and hedges and compel them to come in, that the house may be filled.

The highways represent places that are out in the open and the hedges are where people are hiding because of shame and lack of trust of *anyone*. Yet, there is a compelling factor for them as well. We get to discover how God instructs in compelling the ones He loves, to come and eat at the table He has set for them to taste living water and the bread of life.

Just with this example using the parable Jesus taught us, we can see that not everyone will receive the Truth (Jesus) the same way. There is a compelling factor with each category, and as we go out, God gives us His heart, His compassion, His language, and His insight on how to compel someone to understand God's unconditional love for them.

CONSIDER YOUR FIELD

It's now time to understand that we're living in a "sheep among wolves" reality. We will have to learn to do things differently—to be "wise as serpents and harmless as doves," as Matthew 10:16 says. When I started going to many crazy festivals and events, God spoke to me and said, "Your words aren't my words, your thoughts aren't my thoughts, and your ways are not my ways." My immediate response was, "Lord, teach me *your* ways."

It became clear, that we, the church, have been trained in evangelistic efforts that *used* to work in earlier revival times. But times have changed, and the church has not changed. We expect people to pray with us to receive a Jesus they have no understanding about and quote the magical "sinners' prayer" (which isn't in the Bible, by the way) and make a life-changing decision with us, a stranger, after having a five-minute conversation on the street and hearing a "rapid fix" speech about salvation.

When there is a revival atmosphere in the air, there is freedom to speak more openly about God, but until that is present, we have to listen and learn how God wants to communicate in the season we are in. God began to show me how ineffective this old type of communication is. Not only is it ineffective, but it can also be damaging to a person God may be trying to reach. Please do not misunderstand. I am not running down the church. People in churches have good hearts as they are trying to communicate a life with Jesus to a person who is desperate to hear "good news" and change their lives forever, like we did. As stated before, times have changed. People are living in a false reality where evil is good and good is evil. I think we can all agree that the world we now live in has rapidly changed in regard to culture, beliefs, lifestyle acceptance, and spiritual intolerance. We are in a post-Christ era. We are living in a time where Isaiah 60:1–3 is unfolding before our eyes:

> Arise, shine; for your light has come! And the glory of the Lord is risen upon you. For behold, the darkness shall cover the earth, and deep darkness the people; but the Lord will arise over you, and His glory will be seen upon you. The Gentiles shall come to your light, and kings to the brightness of your rising.

Not everyone thinks like we do as Christians, nor have they had positive experiences while attending church or a religious organization. We are currently living in a world that is convinced largely by a spirit of delusion that causes them to form their own pathways and decisions, and create lives that are completely apart from God. I've often referred to these people as the "God-hardened, Godless, and God-confused."

THE GOD YOU WISH YOU ALWAYS KNEW

The information you will learn will help to create in you a new mindset and understanding of the world we live in. The goal is to teach how we can effectively communicate the same love God has demonstrated to us and to a world that is desperate to know His unconditional love. There are so many misconceptions about the love of God. Jesus told His followers to let Him lead and He would teach them how to reach people. He knows everyone's past, their design, their heart, and their hurt. His whole focus is on restoration and a fulfilled life.

If we are serious about going into all the world and spreading the love of God in every place, we must allow love to conquer fear and insecurity. The Holy Spirit will guide us, teach us, equip us, and download us with wisdom, as well as the power to pave the way for people to return to the One who made them.

Most people's trust bridges are ruined. The basic need and hunger in every human's heart is to know pure love and have a true understanding of how to live life. When we describe Jesus by His character and nature instead of using His name, it provides a safe place for people to allow the actual Giver of Life into their lives and situation without any fear or offense. I believe we have a responsibility to redefine Jesus to a world who does not know who He is. We do this through describing Him by His attributes, character, functions, and nature.

I often think of those four guys in Mark 2 who took the drastic measures of taking their paraplegic friend, who was bedridden, up and through a roof to get him in front of Jesus. Jesus was the only One who could do something about his problem. The more we get out of the way and let God encounter a person, the more creatively He operates. He knows just what each individual one of them needs—after all, He is their

Creator. Our effort is to do the same. Get people in the presence of Jesus, who changes their hearts and lives by way of an encounter with the Holy Spirit, and *then* we explain to them where it came from. Especially *now*. Please don't misunderstand this strategy. We are *not* ashamed of the name of Jesus or the gospel; however, the world who is apart from God has been duped into thinking differently about Jesus than we do. This is where God instructs us how to speak to the one He is reaching and avoid walls coming up and shutting us down.

There is an epidemic of addiction to pornography within the church—leadership included— and with it comes abuse and defilement that wraps victims in shame. I have said many times that the world is watching. God is pulling the cover off. There is a great respect for people who willingly repent because of conviction, not because they got caught. And there is grace extended to anyone who "comes clean."

Anyone who will decide to get help, lay down their pride, and become transparent, God promises to restore. This goes for both the abused and the abuser. The ladies at the porn convention have told us story after story about how they once were involved in church but mishandled, and in many cases abused, from the time they were small. Anyone who calls on the name of the Lord with a sincere heart can come to the mercy seat and be both forgiven and completely transformed.

We also understand porn has reached an epidemic level right now and is only getting more prevalent. People, especially young kids, are being swept into this industry because of the money and perceived success. They are fed a lie about modeling and movies. These hurt kids will do just about anything when they are told how beautiful they are. It is just a frog in the water not knowing the temperature is about to heat up to a deadly level, killing their dreams and spirit.

FIRST STEPS

The very first thing to do is to identify your field. Who are you speaking with and how do they listen and comprehend what the message is God is giving you for them? What is their language and how do you need to communicate the message? Remember, they do not know the Bible and, in most cases, do not give it any credibility for being a source of information. They do not speak "Christianese" or hold to Bible verses.

Using these practiced phrases will most often turn them off, and they will never receive the message. I avoid using words like *Jesus, Christ, Christian, God,* and others. When the Lord told me to go back and read the Gospels, I found out that Jesus didn't use them either. He called God "His Father" and didn't go around telling everyone who He was. In fact, in several instances, I could find He sternly warned people who were healed of leprosy, blindness, and death *not* to say anything at all. In Mark 1:40–45, Jesus heals a leper, and it goes as follows:

> Now a leper came to Him, imploring Him, kneeling down to Him and saying to Him, "If You are willing, You can make me clean." Then Jesus, moved with

compassion, stretched out His hand and touched him, and said to him, "I am willing; be cleansed." As soon as He had spoken, immediately the leprosy left him, and he was cleansed. And He strictly warned him and sent him away at once, and said to him, "See that you say nothing to anyone; but go your way, show yourself to the priest, and offer for your cleansing those things which Moses commanded, as a testimony to them."

When Jesus heals two blind men in Matthew 9:27–30, it goes like this:

When Jesus departed from there, two blind men followed Him, crying out and saying, "Son of David, have mercy on us!" And when He had come into the house, the blind men came to Him. And Jesus said to them, "Do you believe that I am able to do this?" They said to Him, "Yes, Lord." Then He touched their eyes, saying, "According to your faith let it be to you." And their eyes were opened. And Jesus sternly warned them, saying, "See that no one knows it."

The same thing happens when Jesus heals Jairus's daughter in Mark 5:38–43:

Then He came to the house of the ruler of the synagogue, and saw a tumult and those who wept and wailed loudly. When He came in, He said to them,

"Why make this commotion and weep? The child is not dead, but sleeping." And they ridiculed Him. But when He had put them all outside, He took the father and the mother of the child, and those who were with Him, and entered where the child was lying. Then He took the child by the hand, and said to her, "Talitha, cumi," which is translated, "Little girl, I say to you, arise." Immediately the girl arose and walked, for she was twelve years of age. And they were overcome with great amazement. But He commanded them strictly that no one should know it, and said that something should be given her to eat.

Jesus spoke to the multitude in parables or picture language that fit the day. He used words they could relate to, like seeds and wheat. Matthew 13:34 says that "without a parable He did not speak to them."

Despite everything people have embraced instead of Him, Father God loves them deeply, fiercely, and completely. I've now come to know God's "reckless" love. It is reckless because it will go into any pit, porn convention, or pagan festival despite the high risk of rejection.

Everyone's story looks like this. We were once seeking answers to life. For me, I was seeking a way to live life apart from drugs and substance abuse. In churches we've pastored, I've found that we forget this simple yet powerful truth: we were them before we were us. I heard a statement once that we in the church have a problem with those who sin in a different way than we do. When I heard this, it resonated with me so deeply. Our place has never been to judge another person. We have never walked in their shoes and do not know their story.

PRISONERS OF WAR

I don't have to tell you there is real evil in the world and it's out to destroy us. You know that. Satan's schemes are obvious, and his victims are as numerous as the sands of the sea. While there is safety in the church, it was never meant to be a cruise ship. Jesus launched a battleship two thousand years ago, and we are becoming an army of justice fighters who will not back down when the battle gets tough.

He's looking for warriors to armor up and go behind enemy lines. The mission? Search and rescue. We were made to walk into darkness and snatch prisoners of war from the enemy, who has ensnared them with lies, fear, and plenty of accusations. Our teams have forged a pathway into many different arenas, set up camp, and braved extreme places such as the porn convention, pagan festivals, New Age arenas, and anywhere people who live in darkness need the "Light of Life."

What we have discovered in these arenas is that people have been given the wrong version of Jesus. His love is unconditional and non-judgmental, and He is desperately in love with *all* people, regardless of the lifestyles they have chosen to live. There are no limits to His love—no restrictions or disqualifications for tattoos, piercings, shaved heads, prison terms, or number of trips to the gay bar or the divorce attorney.

CHAPTER 3

THREE PRIMARY GROUPS OF CULTURE

Let's break down three primary groups that will give us a starting point to understand the culture and world we are now living in. These are just three groups I have noted so you can have the information, but there are others we will address as you continue to read. They are the God-hardened, the Godless, and the God-confused.

THE GOD-HARDENED

These are typically folks who have had some sort of painful church experience. Either they were raised in church, attended a church, worked in a church, or placed some value on trying to explore what church is in hopes they might find community. In my experience, the God-hardened are the most difficult to reach because their wounding is somehow associated with their ideas of God or His church. We must change our language to prevent triggers from past hurts that could be associated with a bad experience.

Many people I have encountered on outreaches are searching to fill a spiritual hole and have been hurt or devalued in church. They are protective of themselves and tend to plop anyone calling themselves Christian into a bucket of "bad people, bad experiences." Due to their past experiences, they will put up a wall before you ever get a chance to bring hope to them.

This is a huge part of why we change our language. "Church hurt" seems to be the absolute worst hurt of all. It is more damaging than a broken romantic relationship or an abusive childhood experience. When people think they can no longer go to church for help or community, they become vulnerable to every deceptive and demonic trap. When people find hurt or rejection in the very community in which they trust to find hope, healing, and life, a terrible lie is planted in their minds. They will believe that there is no safe place for them.

The devil waits to tell people that God is the cause of their pain. Then, if they go to a church and are rejected, used, or abused by anyone within the church, they tend to harden their hearts toward anything that has even the slightest hint of "God." They are triggered by Christianese language or agendas.

Hurting people hurt people. This is a fact. Churches are full of hurt people who are trying to get better themselves,

THREE PRIMARY GROUPS OF CULTURE

which is so good and yet so challenging at the same time. Over the past few decades, atrocities that have occurred with bad leadership in churches have increased substantially. Sexual abuse at the hands of leaders who prey on hurting people looking for help—pedophilia, assaults on boys and girls, adultery, power-hungry and ego-driven leaders, you name it—has happened within the church. Some leaders have great charisma and popularity to gather a big crowd but are absent of moral conviction. They live from the spark of their own "successes" instead of God's word. By leading like a dictator instead of a shepherd, they have wounded countless people with their wickedness.

We've heard horror stories of "church hurt" experiences. Not all are of sexual nature. Sometimes people just didn't fit in, or they felt betrayed when they trusted someone with something in ill-spent confidence, which blew up a trust bridge and left the betrayed one feeling that is what God is like.

When any such thing happens, a person begins to become God-hardened and distant. So, when you encounter a person who has been through this type of experience and you use the same language as the church that hurt them, the wounded one automatically puts you in the bucket with all of the people they do not trust. This is why we *must* learn to listen to God about how He wants to communicate with them. With this definition, you can see why it is essential for the face and structure of the church to change.

In my outreach efforts to the God-hardened, I've heard story after story of people who have been so completely devastated by their church experience that they have created a wall around their hearts and minds in order to never be hurt like that again. We're finding that a lot of young people are not interested in a church experience at all. They feel like they cannot relate to the current model of church. I've heard many stories from young girls that have come out of "religious cults" about their "spiritual leader" molesting them—even with the support or permission of a parent. Unfortunately, these predators cause great harm emotionally to these young girls, whose parents followed the instructions of the cult to allow such a thing.

Is it any wonder why people have become God-hardened? Most victims would never want to have anything to do with church or a religious organization ever again—unless they were to have a true encounter with their Creator.

Similarly, same-sex relationships are usually formed because people have been burned in past relationships, so they turn to the same sex to be understood and heard. When I've heard their stories, I have been told that we in the church have no interest in listening. We have perfected the art of listening to respond instead of listening to hear. We have largely failed to see people who live different lifestyles as Jesus' friends.

I have heard these stories from people at porn conventions, counterculture events, coffee shops, and even my local grocery store, but the God-hardened aren't always victims of physical abuse. Sometimes, as creatives, they were just not accepted because of their uniqueness. Present-day churches have not been very effective at allowing creatives to express what God has put inside of them.

THREE PRIMARY GROUPS OF CULTURE

These creative ones will be instrumental to introducing a new sound and new expression of the changing church. Because of their sensitive makeup and creative wiring, they were rejected and asked to conform to their church's standards instead of allowing the Holy Spirit to flow through them and birth new expression for this new revival. Pastors' kids often make up a large number of those in this category of powerful creatives. God has invested in them revelation for the coming days.

In the most countercultural "post-Christ" or "anti-Christ" arenas, people have tried church or heard about God and have simply taken the bait of an identity-based lie. Let's discuss another possible reaction—the one where they have decided that they don't need God and that they possibly *are* God rather than trusting in something (or someone) who has allowed them to be hurt. This is called humanism. There has to be a way for us to communicate the love of God to them because He told us to go into all the world and preach the gospel to every creature, not just the ones we decide or choose to go to. Tell me, what part of all of the world are we, the church, supposed to stay out of?

When we understand that darkness covers the earth, and deep darkness covers people and their minds, it becomes clear that rational thinking disappears in the darkness and gives way to a spirit of delusion. It's almost as if a dark cloud settles over the minds of people who are not connected to God. This can also affect people who *are* connected to God. When I've been ministering to a person who is God-hardened, the Lord has opened my eyes to see the stronghold that has settled over their mind. I know it sounds weird, but I can see the anatomy of the brain with black moss covering it, preventing them from understanding or being able to navigate their lives the way they were designed.

If I can have such revelation, so can you—just ask Him for the ability to see His truth of what is in front of you. The deception that has been embraced as reality has clouded their minds and left them trapped in their own "fake world." Second Corinthians 4:3–4 says, "But even if our gospel is veiled, it is veiled to those who are perishing, whose minds the god of this age has blinded, who do not believe, lest the light of the gospel of the glory of Christ, who is the image of God, should shine on them." They have created a false reality to function in life, even though it's far from the truth.

THE GODLESS

The "Godless" are those who have come to the conclusion that there is no God, no heaven, no hell, and no devil. Usually, the idea is that if there is no God, devil, hell, or heaven, then they are not responsible for the eternal consequences of their lives or actions. Once a person understands that God exists, they are faced with the realization that there is some kind of accountability and action needs to be taken on their part. When dealing with the Godless, understand that there is a narcissist mindset attached to their thinking. This usually stems from a fear-based life history that causes a person to shield or protect themselves from any responsibility they may

THREE PRIMARY GROUPS OF CULTURE

take. They use a "blame-shifting" approach to project any ownership of actions of their own onto someone else.

Let's understand that the devil has placed a blinded shield over the minds of people to prevent them from seeing the light of the gospel. If there is a shield over the minds of people to understand light, then there has to be another way in. Yes, we can and do take authority over this blindness, but we first have to earn the trust of that person to even be able to talk to them.

The world doesn't speak "church" words or, as we like to call it, "Christianese." What is Christianese? It's language we have learned from the Bible to communicate with each other. The world we currently live in has become indifferent to the current church model, so they've decided to disconnect from it and now have also distanced themselves from God as well. The Godless are often the most challenging with which to build a bridge of communication. Being heavily guarded in their thinking, they are overly cautious about even engaging in conversation.

This is where dream interpretation comes in. Everyone dreams whether they think they do or not, so asking them if you can interpret a dream for them is usually a safe way to lower a bridge into the life of a person with a Godless mindset. It is especially important to be careful not to use any, and I mean *none*, of the Christianese language with them. They will throw a wall up faster than you can blink.

THE GOD-CONFUSED

The God-confused are spiritually sensitive, but have a myriad of ideas developed into their belief system. In my experience, this mixture develops a twisted combination of all kinds of religions and spiritual experiences and rolls them into a comfortable little package that offers the good, bad, and ugly of various spirits and gods—emphasis on the lowercase "g." They pick and choose what they will believe and usually adhere to the popular phrase, "I believe there are many ways to God."

I have several answers to that statement. Here are some examples I have given to the God-confused: "My daughter is a pilot. With that perception of different pathways, would you or I be able to tell my daughter that there are many ways to safely land a plane, or is there only one way that is designed for planes to land?"

I have also told them, "I also was on a spiritual journey in my early years and had many choices of a spiritual path for myself. In my search, I discovered that there were many spiritual options, all touting supreme spiritual life lands here or here. But I made my own decision that I was not going to surrender my life for someone who did not give their life for me, and there is only one who did that. Jesus." I just told them my story without forcing anything on them.

Jesus told me flat-out, "If you are kind to my friends, I'll introduce you to them." We *must* remember that people are confused and hurting. God helps us see people like He does and realize that people are in the process of coming to the knowledge of both God's existence and also His kindness, which will always lead people to repentance and change (see Romans 2:4).

CHAPTER 4

THE COUNTERCULTURE/ CANCEL CULTURE DILEMMA

These are words we have seldom heard until recent years. What is counterculture? Counterculture is living by your own rules, with a no-standards, free-expression lifestyle. Healthy guidelines for life have been tossed out because they seem restrictive and prevent them from being creative.

What is cancel culture? Cancel culture refers to the popular practice of withdrawing support for (or canceling) public figures and companies after they have said or done something considered objectionable or offensive. This mindset presents an even greater obstacle in creating conversation. We need to be aware of verbal land mines that we could step on unknowingly, which would cause a person who needs to hear truth to wall themselves up and end the conversation.

God began to introduce me to counterculture by way of New Age venues, pagan gatherings, and eventually even more extreme events such as the Burning Man festival, independent film festivals, and adult conventions. Keep in mind that I was completely unfamiliar with any of these arenas. I found Jesus when I was twenty years old and never looked any further for a spiritual path. God had plans for me beyond my wildest imagination. I am a forerunner who has always been drawn off the beaten path to wild places to discover what God had for me.

To put it another way, I have never lived too long in the place or mindset I lovingly call "planet Christian." As I followed His voice, I discovered that people are desperate and hungry for truth—but convincing them Jesus is the "Truth" and the "Bread of Life" often proved much harder when using conventional Christian expressions. Jesus had to be communicated to them in a way they could understand. Here I discovered God wanted to teach me something I had never considered before.

Please keep in mind that we are communicating the gospel in a *different language*. We're speaking the Word of God in a language people outside of church can understand, and avoiding unnecessary spiritual arguments that never go anywhere. This is done by removing the triggering words developed through prejudices and founded on the lies most have developed as a result of being hurt.

This experience gave me a completely new perspective of God's ways, which are so many times not our ways. It also

THE COUNTERCULTURE/CANCEL CULTURE DILEMMA

made me realize how far removed the church was from the world we currently live in. Jesus told us to be *in* the world but not *of* it, but sadly, the church wasn't in the world. We quickly discovered that our absence in culture created a void which was overwhelmingly filled in by a counterfeit spirituality that people ate up.

Just within the New Age culture alone, many psychics, mystics, creatives, and spiritually hungry people had already tried Christianity, found no acceptance in the church, and were frequently rejected from the "box" of church structures. So, they left churches and their spiritual hunger led them to settle for counterfeit spiritual experiences.

People are both hungry for spiritual truth and eager to help others find guidance for their lives. Sadly, they often use information they receive from "other sources" (darkness) instead of Jesus, who is the Truth. One of my first experiences at a New Age workshop was paid for by my boss at the time, who wanted his whole staff to attend the event to become "spiritually enlightened." My boss was what we call a seeker. God was drawing him, but his previous church experience had convinced him that any kind of God relationship was suffocating, overbearing, unwelcoming, and unloving—therefore, he wanted nothing to do with church ever again.

Only I and one other co-worker were Christians. As the weekend started, I felt the Holy Spirit all over me with revelations for people at the same time that tarot card readers and psychics were giving their readings all around me. I began to get prophetic words for people and, unlike those at this workshop, I began giving them without charge. I found myself using language like *energy, light, enlightenment, spiritual cleansing*, and others. When I spoke their basic language, the people there were very receptive to what God wanted to say to them.

As the weekend progressed, the attendees at this workshop began to seek me out for prophetic words over their lives to the point where the psychics were losing business. It was awkward for me, but I took notice of the accuracy of the words of knowledge God was giving me and the overwhelming presence of God with me. Others could feel it too, even though they didn't know what it was—it was tangible and powerful. I also discovered that God was not "mad" at these people. He was (and is) fully aware of their seeking journey. He knows how to reach the ones He loves so much and sent Jesus to die for.

That was really my first calling card from God. He is not afraid to go into these places that we are afraid of. He is already there. He has superior power. While we have knowledge, we also have everything because God gives us everything.

Like I said before, I'm a forerunner. I always seem to do things first. I think God picked me to lead the way so everyone else can get a look at it before they leap. He said to me, "Do not be afraid to share your story with people because I know there are a lot of people, particularly women in ministry, who have felt suffocated—that they have not felt like they had a voice. They have not felt like they could accomplish anything."

I had just been through that territory and lived to tell the tale. I now had a burning desire to go into those places and situations where God could use me most, no matter where they were.

CHAPTER 5

THE POWER OF DREAMS

Dreams are God's idea. People have often told me that dreams are New Age practices, but I always bring them back to the author of dreams: God. It started in Genesis and we can confidently say that one-third of the Bible is made up of dreams and visions. The entire book of Revelation is an open vision.

God puts much importance on dreams. We know this because that was the way He chose to communicate with Joseph, Jesus' earthly father, when Mary was pregnant with Jesus, which you can read about in the first two chapters of Matthew. Jesus' entire birth and protection was communicated to Joseph by having three dreams. The dreams told Joseph how to navigate the second most important event since the creation of the universe. Think about it: if God used dreams as a vital communication source during such an important time as the birth of Jesus, we can conclude that God puts much more weight on the vehicle of dreams than we do. I address the importance of dreams in my book, *What Your Dreams Are Telling You: Unlocking Solutions While You Sleep.*

Often the best way to reach people (including those who are wounded by a life apart from God) is by way of dream interpretation. With their having already received a message in the night while they sleep, we have an opportunity to help them understand that message, and that it is likely from a divine source. This also diverts them from going to a psychic for an interpretation that would surely push them further off the path to their identity and destiny. Dreams belong to God, and He tells us exactly what He uses them to accomplish. Job 33:14–18 says:

> For God may speak in one way, or in another, yet man does not perceive it. In a dream, in a vision of the night, when deep sleep falls upon men, while slumbering on their beds, then He opens the ears of men, and seals their instruction. In order to turn man from his deed, and conceal pride from man, He keeps back his soul from the Pit, and his life from perishing by the sword.

God says He opens our ears to give us instruction, turn us from doing wrong, and keep us from arrogant thinking, physical harm, and eternal separation from Him. That makes dreams very important. For centuries, the Lord has been using dreams to speak into His friends. But many miss the message or don't know what it means. That's why dream interpretation is a great tool to reach this seeker generation. We need more people trained and gifted in this arena. I'm talking about the Daniels and Josephs who need to rise up in this critical time. As Job 33:23–25 says:

> If there is a messenger for him, a mediator, one among a thousand, to show man His uprightness, then He is gracious to him, and says, 'Deliver him from going down to the Pit; I have found a ransom;' His flesh shall be young like a child's. He shall return to the days of his youth.

That's the power of Holy Ghost dream interpretation: deliverance from darkness and restoration to God's original intent for each dreamer. They feel like a kid again and their passion is restored when they understand what their Maker is saying to them. I am thrilled that I am one of a thousand messengers and mediators rising up in wise counsel. I can honestly tell you that interpreting dreams is some of the most important and fulfilling work I've done for the Kingdom.

Our teams consider dream interpretation a big part of our outreach efforts and have proven that helping people understand a message they've had in a dream is rewarding for the dreamer as well as our team members. Dreams are fascinating, and people most often feel valued when they are listened to in the telling of a dream.

SUNDANCE FILM FESTIVAL AND THE DREAM DOCUMENTARY IN THE MAKING

I always want to be flexible and ready for the latest call of the Lord, so when He told me I was going to take a team to the Sundance Film Festival in Park City, Utah, I was ready to jump in. I knew Utah well after living there for several years.

Just like New Age festivals, Burning Man, and porn conventions, Sundance is overflowing with the creatives and countercultural trendsetters. Cinematographers, writers, set and costume designers, actors, and directors are everywhere. These people think differently. They see the world in different and more varied colors and from a myriad of perspectives. Their imaginations are ten steps ahead of ours. I find this sad because those of us connected to the Creator should be the most creative people on the planet, but we aren't because we've latched onto rules and boxes. We've given that ground to the enemy and God wants us to take it back.

It was 2001 and Sundance that year was in full swing. We had not begun outreach efforts to the festival yet, so I was just attending with my two daughters. A young man walked up to us and asked me if we would like tickets to a show that was extremely sexual by title description. Unfortunately, at that point I did not have the training I'm sharing with you now, so I was appalled. I looked straight at him, got really close to his face, and said, "Do I *look* like I want to see a movie about that?" He backed up, quietly said, "No, I don't think you do," and took off down the street.

My daughters were watching me, and I told them we were going to eat. We walked into the nearby restaurant on Main Street and the servers sat us at the back of the restaurant. We had a full view to everyone in there, all of whom were part of the film industry and sat at tables with their credentials around their necks.

The Lord suddenly brought me into a prophetic experience, in which they all turned and looked at me at the same time. I could see the brokenness behind their faces and the image they tried to portray. They were empty and sad, with nothing to offer that would benefit an audience on a big screen. Their films reflected the emptiness and nothingness inside them.

I stood up in the restaurant because the experience was so real and shouted, "Where is the prophetic church?" Immediately God spoke to me and said, "The prophetic church is inside the church." My daughters were completely horrified and told me to sit down. Thankfully, the restaurant was very loud and crowded, so no one really saw me do that except my daughters.

After that, I was determined to create outreach teams to the festival and reach into the hearts of people who were making movies that everyone was watching. What they were creating was contributing to the moral decline of our nation, the world, and our young people.

Dreams were the answer. We discovered that this popular

festival was filled with dreamers, literally. Many of the film makers had received the idea for their film through a dream. It was a perfect fit.

Now, for ten cold winter days in Park City, we walk the streets and find impactful ways to engage with these crazy creatives when nobody else does. But first, we decided we would try to blend in a little. Over the span of eight years, our outreach teams grew to as many as fifty dream interpreters for the four-day festival. People came to help us from California, Texas, New Jersey, Montana, and Florida, and one couple came from Scotland.

One year, I went into a store to interpret a dream of the woman behind the counter. She asked what we were doing at the festival this year, assuming that we might have had a film in the festival. Without thinking, I immediately blurted out, "We are making a documentary about dreams."

I heard God say to me, "Oh, are you?"

I answered silently, thoughtfully, "Well, yes."

After all, we were out there among the movie makers. A lot of dreams are embedded into movies. We considered it a shoo-in. We had no idea how to make a movie, but there we were, camera in hand, working around professional, independent film makers—people who definitely knew how to make a documentary.

Thanks to a team member who offered to buy it if we paid him back later, we purchased a professional-grade camera. Without a clue of what to do or how to use it, we stumbled on a teaching session for filmmakers and wandered in.

THE POWER OF DREAMS

As I was looking about the room, my heart nearly came to a stop. I spotted the team member who paid for the camera sitting on stage as a member of the speaking panel for filmmaking professionals, which he knew nothing about. He had never made a film in his life! Even though our friend could sell ice to an Alaskan on a winter day, I was pretty certain he had absolutely no experience creating videos, movies, or film clips at all.

Yet here he was, answering questions on the panel for filmmakers at Sundance Film Festival. One thing was obvious: he had a prophetic anointing on him, and I believe that's what got him through that session. Nobody suspected he was clueless, and he even began to sound like an expert! When questioned who we were and what we were doing there, we said we were with him, hoping we would not be removed for any reason.

Later that evening, we crashed a private food and wine party. I greeted the security guard at the door and said, "Oh my gosh. It is so good to see you again!" He was not supposed to let people in without an invitation, so I kept talking: "It has been like a year and—oh, my goodness! There is Frank!" With that, I walked through the door with my team following me. We walked right in like we owned the place, ate some food, and interpreted their dreams—having fun rubbing elbows with who knows who.

We had no true credentials. The ones we did have were fake, made to look similar to others that people wore at

Sundance. My whole outreach ministry has been like this. We just try stuff. When God has an appointment or assignment, He will make a way for you. It is the truth.

We were surrounded by independent filmmakers, movie stars, and people you would easily know from the movies or television. We would walk down the street in the cold and interpret their dreams. The Holy Spirit would show up, and those just passing by would stop and listen to the dream and its interpretation. We quickly started to draw a crowd, which was not a good thing because we were such amateurs. At one point, no joke, we had the camera upside down. We did not know what we were doing at all. We were dream interpreters, not filmmakers.

Still, we captured it all on film. It was so wonderful. People were literally getting rocked by the Holy Spirit's interpretation of their dreams. Dreams and their meaning belong to God. So, I thought, *If they belong to Him, they are accessible to us, right?* We continued interpreting dreams throughout the festival.

When the festival was over, we had so much footage, it was ridiculous! Despite not having a clue about what we were doing, everything miraculously all came together. We actually produced our dream interpretation documentary. We submitted it to Sundance, but they turned it down. It is called *Dreams, a Documentary* and is downloadable at CindyMcGill.org.

Now, not everyone believes the same way we do about God or Jesus. They have a different idea and definition of Him. They think He is something other than what He is. We are very careful about how He wants us to communicate. Keeping that in mind when Sundance turned us down, we decided we would just rent a screen ourselves and show the film during the festival. God gave us favor to do it. He made it happen because we didn't have any connections. When looking for a screen to show it on, we were told by a complete stranger, "I have an open screen at six o'clock on Thursday. I'll just charge you five hundred dollars if you want to show your film."

Boy, did we! We didn't charge admission. We made posters and put them up and down the streets of Sundance. We had lines and lines of people waiting to get in. Miraculously, after folks saw it the first time, they brought their friends back to see it a second time. We did not have enough room in the theater for all of them because there were so many. Some were blocking the foyer.

Better yet, we even had people going to the Sundance box office to get tickets to a movie that Sundance had turned down! The people in the box office were wondering who we were and what this mystery movie people wanted tickets for was all about. The Sundance people started asking questions and trying to track us down! Talk about the power of God. Sundance was coming after us.

Several movie producers saw our film and told us, "This documentary probably will not really ever go anywhere because of the poor editing, the uneven lighting, and the volume," along with plenty of other issues. They had a long list of what we did wrong. While they were talking to us about it being a bomb, our producer/director got a call from Hollywood. Our movie had just been selected for First Glance Hollywood. On top of that, it had won an award for—wait for it—editing!

In all, our dream interpretation film went on to win other awards from all over the world: Ireland, Egypt, Hollywood, Hawaii, Mexico, the United Kingdom, and Phoenix, Arizona. That is just how God works. We figure that He is God. We just like to see Him be God and do whatever He wants to do because it's always better than anything we could dream up ourselves.

CHAPTER 6

USING WORDS THAT WORK AT OUTREACH EVENTS

We just gave you a look into our outreach at the Sundance Film Festival, where dreams and their interpretations were the most effective way to reach the people in that arena. Now we want to describe for you some of the other festivals and events where we have attended annually and used the language that you will learn in this book.

THE BURNING MAN FESTIVAL

Who knew there was an annual festival in the middle of the Nevada desert where the creatives, mystics, seekers, and sojourners met for two weeks and lived out their fantasy lives? I didn't have a clue. At Burning Man, I found people of all ages and backgrounds shedding their "skin" in this non-judgmental atmosphere. No hiding behind masks of convention and business suits to fit into the collective of society. Just folks being their true selves, whatever that truth happened to be, with no explanation necessary. It is a vastly different, creative space that has become somewhat of an urban legend.

Many who attend are incredibly creative. They craft their art and generate imaginative projects on what they call the Playa, which means the beach. Some years, the festival holds more than eighty-five thousand people just trying to be true to themselves. They look for truth without ever knowing they're actually searching for the One who made them.

I was pretty wild as a young person before meeting the Lord, but nothing prepared me for the desire God put on my heart for the lost. I first started going to Burning Man in 2003. What I experienced those initial ten days in the middle of the Black Rock Desert was thousands of young people living a free-expression lifestyle. It was like a world I had never imagined before. These were not only the creatives, but they were also the visionaries—the influencers of today—from youthful internet billionaires to heads of companies like Google, Wired, Rolling Stone, and the dot-coms we all know and use.

People who attend and invest in this festival embrace the ideology of entitlement and moral relativism. We have been given the access into this world since the early 2000s because God wanted us to see what was coming—the present-day world we live in—so we could be educated and equipped to communicate with them. This way, they could have an

USING WORDS THAT WORK AT OUTREACH EVENTS

encounter with God and Holy Spirit in a safe place, bypassing their mindsets and experiencing God for themselves.

Using the strategies that God gave us, these people were able to encounter God free of the church structure, phraseology, and stereotypes that they found so appalling. In fact, one year there was an art display on the Playa that was called "The Church Trap." It looked like a church with a pole holding it up in the air, similar to what a mouse trap would look like. Inside the art piece sat an organ, sheet music, a cross, and pews. The artist revealed the festival goers' irreverence and disappointment for traditional church. They considered church to be a trap that offered them nothing but shame and guilt, so they wanted to get away from it.

When you see this type of art piece featured at an event, it speaks volumes about how they perceive Jesus, God, and anything associated with church as nothing more than a trap to rob them of their creativity and individuality. God told us to change our language so that we could communicate with people who held onto this mindset.

At least once a year, people come together to form a free-thinking community made up of theme camps where everyone is on the same level. These camps are diverse in expression and sectioned off into free-flowing societies within their boundaries. There are certain spirit camps, camps given over to sexual experiences, rave camps with parties that last all night long, and just about any kind of creative expression you could imagine.

The entire short-lived metropolis is built around the giant

effigy of a man who stands at least one hundred feet in the air. That's ten stories tall. The Burning Man is made of wood, which is set ablaze at the end of the event in celebration of the Burners' experiences. In the center is a temple for worship of any and all "gods." While most Christians would cringe at the idolatry inside, the temple actually made it easier for us to invite seekers to our camp because they were already looking for a spiritual experience. We thought that we might as well give them one! We undercover Jesus freaks would go in while people were meditating, weeping, participating in seances or New Age practices, and present ourselves as "heart healers" and "healing artists." It was the truth. We were there to heal their hearts and let the true creative Artist of the universe work through us. Boy, did He show up!

THE TEMPLE

The giant temple on the complex is designed to give people a spiritual place to release their pain and connect with their inner self. This structure works really well for us because it was completely acceptable to go in while people were meditating, grieving, or taking part in a seance or New Age cleansing ritual, and act as truth finders, heart healers, and healing artists.

At the temple, the Burners write tributes all over the walls because they are going to burn it down anyway. It is their version of confession—a way of letting go of past hurt and failure. We saw messages like:

"I'm sorry I killed you."

"I'm sorry I aborted my baby."

"I'm sorry I let you down. I wasn't there when you needed me."

"I miss my mom."

"I miss my friend."

"I am lost."

We have even seen death certificates of those who took their own lives. Whatever caused them to lose hope or impact the life of the person leaving the message, it was there. I thought, *Oh my goodness. Somebody is onto something. This place is a revelation of their hearts, and we have to be able to tune ourselves to listen.* What were they hungry for? What did they have need of? We wanted to know. One year, so many of the writings said, "I miss my grandma," or "My grandmother died this year and I need her." Over and over again, these sojourners were crying out for their grandmothers. They needed that clean, assuring, steady love.

After going to the temple and seeing this pattern, I thought we should have a granny tent. We could have rocking chairs and give them cookies and love. We could give them hugs and speak words of encouragement and comfort to them, connect them to their true identity and calling. We could try it. If nothing else, we had something nice to sit in for the rest of our time there. It was powerful and cathartic to say the least.

Every year, Caleb, one of my team members, went into the temple with his worship flags. I'm talking about the beautiful banners you see at Pentecostal churches where they dance through movement and expression. Caleb is a tall, expressive, powerful man in his forties with a very athletic build. He's a true man of God who was made for battle in creative worship.

When we entered the temple, there was a heavy spirit of grief, sadness, and defeat. Saying it was oppressive would be an understatement. Caleb started twirling his flags in the center of the temple. I don't know if it was the color, the movement of the air, or the crazy joy of it all, but it literally began changing the atmosphere. Suddenly, there was joy where there had been mourning and beauty where there had been ashes. People who had been crying were now laughing.

One of my team members looked up and noticed that the light and the shadow from Caleb's flags was making a pattern on the ceiling of the temple several stories above us. They started pointing for people to look up. Suddenly, everyone was pointing up. They started laughing, proclaiming that there were angels in the room. The Holy Spirit was swirling right along with the flags, and people truly encountered God. He was connecting with His friends in an amazing way. We don't know if anyone got saved in that moment, but that's not always what it's about. It's about opening up opportunities for the Lord to present Himself again and again until they grasp the reality of Him.

People were coming out of trances and flopping over after the temple experience. Guards were there with walkie-talkies, saying, "We need to call in medical help. We have people passing out from the heat." Someone on our team told Caleb that the

USING WORDS THAT WORK AT OUTREACH EVENTS

guards were getting ready to call the paramedics, so he walked over and said, "I think they are okay. This is a spiritual moment."

Then our team got around the people who had fallen out in the spirit and gave them power encounters with the Holy Ghost by praying in tongues over them. It was so powerful and so well received that the coordinators of Burning Man came by, asking, "Who are you? We keep hearing about you."

THE FREEDOM LOUNGE

If you travel to a foreign country, it is very helpful if you learn the culture or attempt to learn the language. That is pretty much what we did. When we set up camp for the first time, we decided the best way to reach this eclectic crowd was to name our camp the "Freedom Lounge" because it described them getting free from anything that might be holding them back or keeping them imprisoned in their current lifestyle. Where the Spirit of the Lord is, there is freedom. We gave the Holy Spirit the freedom to move the way He wanted to at our camp.

We always gave God great room in our marked-off spot at Burning Man. Whatever real estate we had, we always declared it holy unto the Lord. We declared every person that stepped foot on it as set apart for Him, even if they didn't know it yet. Every time, we told the Holy Spirit we were open to anything He wanted to do and that He had complete control over that place.

As He has done so many times over the years, the Lord began to give me the right language for the diverse people who entered our camp, as well as other means of identifying their needs. I actually got a download from God about His language when I went to a Native American reservation in Coeur d'Alene, Idaho. He visited me in the night and an angel met me in the morning, and they gave me instructions on what to do and how to talk to His friends.

The Freedom Lounge became the result of the directions I received in this visitation. I was instructed by the angel to make a "menu board" and little booths with things such as spiritual readings, dream interpretation, healings, and miracles. Using the language God gave me, we created a menu board with certain encounters, using language like "Organic Restart—welcome to your new life." That meant salvation. We did "Original Root Recovery—who are you?" That meant connecting with your true identity. One of the most popular booths was for "Spiritual Cleansing and Redefinement," which meant deliverance.

Between these booths, I had intercessors who did nothing but pray in the Spirit during the encounter. To the seekers, people speaking in tongues is not scary or odd. We just tell them it's a "spirit language" that connects us to the "Creator." They are perfectly fine with that verbiage. God had it all lined up. God told me to call the intercessors "spiritual connectors" who connect us in the Spirit realm.

The downloads came hard and fast, as did the language we were to use. God told me to identify Him by His attributes instead of by His name. He gave these instructions because people think totally differently about the words *God*, *Jesus*,

USING WORDS THAT WORK AT OUTREACH EVENTS

and *Holy Spirit* than we do. Hearing these names of God often walls them up, and they miss the encounter that God wanted to use to reveal Himself to them.

Instead, we call Him the Giver of Life.
We call Him Mercy.
We call Him Comfort.
We call Him Healer.
We call Him Creator.
We call Him Counselor.
We call him Shame Taker.
We call Him the Spirit of Truth.
We call Him Love—the Lover of your heart, the Lover of your soul.
We call Him the One who can restore.
We call Him the One who can bring life.

Mostly, we call Him the Spirit of Truth who opens up the "Way" to give us "Life." All this language makes sense to spiritually hungry people. That is what we call "scratching the itch."

God told me I needed to sound like Him when I talked to His kids. People in the world do not understand church words. It does no good to speak Scripture to them because they do not value it. God told us to identify Him by His unconditional love for them and to treat them with respect and honor.

CHAPTER 7

NEW LANGUAGE TO REACH THE SEEKERS

These are the terms we have used time and again to explain God's transformative work in the world and seekers' lives. All their triggers and negative connotations of Christianese disappear, and they are able to look at salvation and spiritual cleansing positively. At Burning Man, we put these words on a menu board in our tent and seekers can choose what they would like to experience based on their spiritual need. Here's the first language change: don't call people "the lost," not even among your Christian friends or outreach team. Call them seekers. We do this because seekers always find.

ORGANIC RESTART

This is salvation. When people encounter the Holy Spirit (or Spirit of Truth), they feel God's presence for the first time and want to know what it is. We can then explain God and Jesus to them. People come in needing a brand-new place to start their life, healed from their trauma and all they had compromised in their lives. This Organic Restart is a joyful invitation to a new beginning when someone wants a complete life change.

When people express that they want to change their life after encountering the Holy Spirit, understand that they have a misconception of their identity and many times aren't sure of what their purpose is. When someone talks about changing their ways, we start by encouraging them according to their true identity rather than the one they've settled for.

"Let's find the best version of yourself," we can say. "What were you designed for? It's all organic! Let's get you with your gifting and look at what you were made for."

We speak words of life and encouragement to them and ask the Spirit of Truth to organically restart their inner self. Once their identity is restarted and realigned with the Spirit of Truth, everything else will fall into place.

Now that they've had an encounter with Jesus and have felt the presence and power of the One who is so radically in love with them, how could they not want to have a transformed life? He is the One who wants to see you completely whole, healed, redesigned, and realigned, to birth you into your real identity!

Almost 90 percent of the time, people would say, "What just happened to me?" I would respond, "You just had an encounter with the One who made you." They would say "I feel as if I am free," "A ton of weight just dropped off my back,"

"I feel like my lungs are open," "I can see," "Something is new," or "How do I get this?" I would say, "Jesus is the way. That is where my power comes from." We had bottles of water to pour on their head as a form of baptism or outer cleansing once they invited Jesus into their heart. So free, they come back the next day and bring their friends. Whenever we go to Burning Man, our tent is almost always full. Seekers would always look for us because we had something no one else gave them.

ORGANIC SPIRITUAL ALIGNMENT

One of the biggest draws to the Freedom Lounge was what we named "Organic Spiritual Alignment." The Lord showed me that this aligns people with the Holy Spirit, whom we give free rein to move. It is amazing to see. It is so popular that most folks ask for it when they come in. Everything we receive from God is by invitation. When people ask, they receive.

During Organic Spiritual Alignment, they meet Jesus as we prophesy over them what the Holy Spirit tells us to say. We speak identity, purpose, and destiny into them with words of encouragement, comfort, and strength. Think of it like a spiritual chiropractic adjustment, which aligns people into a position to experience God's presence. When the Word of Truth hits them, they are never the same.

We have had so many people experience the Holy Spirit through this "alignment." They were starving for identity and direction, asking, "What do you see about me? Can you give me some understanding or guidance?" We had more people coming to our camp than we had team members to help them. Once they were in an encounter with the Spirit of Truth, there really wasn't much for us to do. God took over.

ORIGINAL ROOT RECOVERY

Original Root Recovery is all about identity. We talk about it when someone has based his or her identity on a traumatic experience. Who are you? What happened when you were two or three years old, when all these other things began to define your life that were contrary to who you really are as a person? What voices gave you false pathways to walk in or images about yourself? Did it take you in a direction you were not meant to go? What happened that hardened your heart or challenged your identity?

It's important to understand that the ones who are attacked by the enemy early on in life are usually appointed by God to make a great difference in this world.

First, acknowledge the person's bad experience and the trauma that it caused.

Reveal the wrong conclusions and identity that have been attached to their good soil.

Encourage them that they are able to recover their original roots, just like weeding a garden. The weeds that don't belong (trauma and old identity) can be taken out of the good soil (their hearts and minds).

Encourage them that the bad roots can be cut off and they can rediscover how the Creator has made them. They can rediscover the true and organic roots that have been

NEW LANGUAGE TO REACH THE SEEKERS

suffocated by the bad roots. Once the bad roots come out, the healthy plants are able to grow and they will discover their true identity and purpose.

Tell them that these bad roots are a lie. They didn't "deserve" to experience the trauma. Say, "This is not who you are. The enemy planted the bad roots to snuff you out and give you a false identity because you are worth so much. You've got such an important part to play."

Once they understand that those roots will be severed and removed, tell them that they now need to protect the garden of their heart fiercely and diligently. Out of their heart will flow the issues of life, like the way they see themselves, the way they see the world, and the contribution they have to this life.

When the Spirit of Truth takes them back to those places, so much is exposed. He speaks these words directly into them:

Here is your original root.

Here is what you were meant to do.

Here is who you are.

Here is what your identity is.

Here is how you are designed.

God would give us specific words of knowledge on how He knit these seekers together, and we would communicate it in ways they could understand. "Here is what I see about you," we would say. When they would ask me how I knew, I would tell them, "I just listened to the One that put you together. He created you and has always known what you were made for. He knows every hair on your head and every word before you speak it. He is intimately acquainted with your ways and knows exactly what your purpose is on this earth and wants to restore you to fulfill your original purpose which only you can do."

There were several others on the team who operated in the "seer gift." We were able to look into the hearts of these seekers, and Jesus would give us a picture of their entire life. I was able to see specific dates as well as the year these events happened. I could look at their heart and see how old they were when deception crept into their heart and misguided their path. Then, I would prophetically place my hand where every radical root system growing out of their heart could be, and I supernaturally cut it off while asking "The Way" (another name for Jesus) to give them direction and take over the places where I saw these unhealthy root systems growing.

Through these Holy Spirit encounters, we were able help them navigate toward wholeness from places where the lives they believed had yanked them off course, even as young children.

When I would call on the Spirit of Truth, some would ask me if I meant God. I would always answer, "Yes, I call Him God." Having understood their mindset and perception of the word *God*, I could tell them what I believed but did not force anything on anyone. Some would tell me they did not believe in God. To that I would say, "I had that option too, and I have made my choice to call Him God." I would add that it was their journey, not mine, and they have the same choice. That's the beauty of free will. God gave us free will as a gift to

NEW LANGUAGE TO REACH THE SEEKERS

use to find Him. What I've found is that most truly are seeking Him, and in His time, He will show Himself to them.

Another thing I would tell these inquisitive Burners is that "I am a follower of Jesus." I never call myself by the label of "Christian" because that puts up a wall. Sadly, any variant of the word *Christian* is now a trigger word for a generation that has experienced the worst of what religion has to offer.

Religious people are the ones who challenged Jesus, and they are ones He had to rebuke because of their stiff-minded ideas. We heard stories from so many people who had been scorned, hurt, shamed, and not valued by "religious" people in their lives. Parents, pastors, people within the church, and leaders of church groups had been cold and unforgiving toward those who were desperately seeking help to change their lives.

These seekers came in many packages, from addicts trapped in every kind of addiction to people who had been sexually abused by someone they trusted. Negative actions from religious people convinced them that Jesus felt the same way about them. This one of the main tools of the devil is to keep people bound by lies in their minds, which harden their hearts toward anyone who labels themselves a "Christian."

Our whole goal in evangelism is to define Jesus the way He *really* is and transform someone's experience with a hurtful religious person. There are certain words, phrases, or names we initially try to stay away from, until they have an encounter with the "Spirit of Truth" or Holy Spirit in order to help them remain open to God's work. Once they have an encounter, they are completely open to know what just happened to them and where it came from. At first, it bothered me not to call Jesus by His name all the time, but when I went back and examined Scripture, I realize Jesus did not even call Himself Jesus. Matthew 16:13–16 tells the following story:

> When Jesus came into the region of Caesarea Philippi, He asked His disciples, saying, "Who do men say that I, the Son of Man, am?" So they said, "Some say John the Baptist, some Elijah, and others Jeremiah or one of the prophets." He said to them, "But who do you say that I am?" Simon Peter answered and said, "You are the Christ, the Son of the living God." Those who spend time with Him *know* who He is.

Earlier in this book, I identified in Scripture where Jesus healed blind people and lepers and raised Jairus's daughter from the dead. In each case, He sternly warned them not to tell people about Him healing them. It was never about fame or credit, rather compassion and relationship.

TRUE REFLECTIONS

Another method we use is called "True Reflections." The purpose of this outreach tool is to help define a new identity for someone who has lived their whole life trying to fit a mold or definition that was never made for them. It's easy and fun to do. You hold up a five-dollar mirror from Walmart and have them sit in front of it. Ask them to look at the mirror and tell themselves everything they see about themselves every day when they look in the mirror.

You stand with the mirror and use kind, affirming words that give hope and reveal their true identity. You call out their gifting and address their woundedness with healing words spoken right to their spirit. Have them repeat the "life" words over themselves. Life always swallows up death.

"What do you see?" we ask. It's heartbreaking the things that come out of the mouths of men and women alike.

"I see a loser."

"I see a fat person who nobody could ever love."

"I see a man instead of a woman."

"I see a liar, a cheat, and a fraud. It's no wonder my life is a mess."

I'm too this, not enough that. The lies and baggage they carry have bogged them down and haunted them all their lives. It's like wearing a backpack and letting everyone who has something negative to say put a rock in that backpack. It would soon become a terrible and painful burden.

After they tell us their identity based on their own understanding, we ask the Spirit of Truth to give us words of knowledge to share with them. Let me tell you, these God-downloads are fast and effective. These words are often so specific to their lives that they ask, "How did you know this? You couldn't possibly know this. I've never told anyone that's my dream."

The Spirit of prophecy is so powerful. People often weep as a whole new image is being created for them. It is our hope that every time they look in a mirror after that, our words of life and identity from the Spirit of Truth are what they see—whenever they look in the mirror, they see a beautiful new identity.

I believe lack of identity is the biggest problem these last two or three generations face. People caught up in self-worship and New Age philosophies have no idea who they were created to be because they have no idea who the Creator is. They are easily deceived by culture, careless words spoken by others, and condemnation they heap upon themselves.

We've all done it. We've believed the lies of the enemy, and it leads to nowhere good. Identity is paramount to our destiny. It's amazing that we can turn years of lies around with nothing more than a five-dollar mirror.

This method of identity recovery did not just work at places like New Age festivals and Burning Man. We also did True Reflections at art festivals in Southern California. We called it "word art" when the event coordinators wanted to kick us out.

While other artists displayed their creations on easels, we had five mirrors set up around our area. There, we created identity and purpose just like Jesus did: with the Living Word. It is so powerful every time we have done this. People are literally transformed into their true identity instead of the one they have settled for. God is so amazing in giving us creative language and words of knowledge to speak to them. It's very personal to each of them. We always have lines of people waiting to have their identity discovered through True Reflections.

LABEL REMOVAL

So often we walk around life with invisible yet destructive labels on us. These are labels we've embraced from the mouths of people who only point out our weaknesses. Label removal is taking spoken negative words off people, even words from early childhood.

As we are looking at a person, God shows us words that have been spoken over them and were used to shape their identity in a negative way. We would call out words God showed us, reach out, and prophetically take the label off them and replace it with the positive word. For instance, if we saw a label that said "failure," we would reach our hand out without touching them and remove the invisible "failure" label and replace it with "success."

Because we know that the power of life and death is in the tongue, speaking life words cancels out death words and the freedom that accompanies the prophetic act becomes clear. Often, people just breathe a sigh of relief.

HEALING FROM THE GREAT PHYSICIAN

This is physical healing from a literal illness. Healing is very common on our outreaches. We visibly watch healing happen or the person with an illness we cannot see tells us that they felt a change inside of their body. When the Holy Spirit has freedom to do what He wants, healings just happen.

For instance, a man came to our camp and was sitting in the waiting area for a seat to open for him to have his encounter. While he was waiting, I noticed him right away and told our greeter, whose job is to walk newcomers to the available spot back to us, that I wanted the "dead" guy. I had never used that phrase before. The greeter intuitively knew who I was speaking of and brought the man back to our little group.

As the man sat down, I noticed he had turned pale and was struggling to breathe. Instantly, I said to him, "I need to put my hand on your hea—"

The man finished my sentence. He said, "I know, I know," and he took my hand and put it on his heart. Our visitor was beginning to have a heart attack. When I put my hand on his heart, I felt the healing power of God flowing through him. Instantly, he was healed.

The very next year at Burning Man, our camp was in a different location on the other side of the Playa. After we set up our camp and as we were having dinner, I started telling that story to my teammates. As I looked up, the man I was talking about was walking right past our camp. I ran out and brought him in. I asked him to tell my team what had happened the year before. He said, "She saved my life. I was having a heart attack, and she put her hand on me and it stopped. I haven't had any heart trouble since that time."

I explained to him that I didn't heal him, but Jesus *did*. He was so thankful we were there at that moment to heal him. Not only was the man healed supernaturally by the Healer, but the very next year, in a completely new location, he walked by our camp at the very moment I was telling a new team about him. You can't make this stuff up. The Holy Spirit is faithful to work through us when we give our lives and actions over to what He wants to do.

WHITE LIGHT SPECIALS

This is our exercise of bringing people out of darkness into light. It is all about revelation and repentance. Truth be told, we really never know what God wants to do during White Light Specials. "The Light" has full freedom to do anything He needs to do to bring them out of the darkness and into freedom.

When we offer a White Light Special, we ask the seeker to envision what they want from the spiritual encounter. The Holy Spirit then connects with them, and their response to this sacred inflow is very often quite intense. Some shake uncontrollably, some cry and sob, some laugh hysterically, and some experience an incredible peace washing over them, transforming them during the encounter. One thing they all tell me is that they feel "touched" and not in a bad way, but a clean way. They feel known and loved, like something in their life has shifted for the better.

In the end, we've moved them one step closer to a real encounter with Jesus. Once they give Him permission to speak into their lives, He can love them in a way they've never known. He is so gentle and kind in how He starts a relationship. He waits until they open the door to Him. Once that door is open, they will never be the same.

HEALING WITH LIGHT AND SOUND

Sound and light travel at the same frequency, and have been found to be a healing tool both physically and spiritually. Music brings supernatural access to the table as we connect with these spirit seekers. Sound opens doors for the Holy Spirit to enter and closes doors the enemy uses to steal, kill, and destroy.

Light, too, heals their deep places. My team and I are always giving the "Spirit of Truth" or "The Light" freedom to bring a person into divine healing and restoration. Using these terms for God is helpful because seekers have a deep metaphysical understanding of what the words mean, even though they don't know Jesus is the Light of the World. They have no idea that He created their entire destiny with just the sound of His voice.

One testimony of a seeker who came to our booth and saw his life begin to transform through sound healing goes as follows: "I went in yesterday and chose 'healing by sound.' If I had not experienced it myself, I would not have thought it actually existed. I am still, and I will always be, changed. I highly recommend it. If you get the chance, go in there. It is crazy."

Sometimes, trauma bonds are broken. Other times, physical healing occurs or emotional wounds from abuse are healed. Regardless of their need for healing, we would always step back and allow the Spirit to do whatever He wanted and use whichever instrument He asked us to use. Most often, the seeker would choose a drum, an Irish whistle, or a didgeridoo. We would just give our best and create a sound that connected them to the Holy Spirit.

My team sees deep, deep healings when we make room for God to do His work. I feel like we are just spiritual midwives and God is the one birthing and restoring these lives.

NEW LANGUAGE TO REACH THE SEEKERS

There are times I call "Hands-Off Encounters," where the Holy Spirit did all the work and we just operated as heaven's "barkers," calling people into the tent.

That's how willing God is to work out a true encounter with His friends. We never know who He is already working with. Many times, Jesus has been working in the life of a seeker for months or years and we're simply the straw that breaks their resistance. I love it when that happens!

SPIRITUAL CLEANSING AND REDEFINEMENT (DELIVERANCE AND SALVATION)

No one can have spiritual cleansing without redefinement. If someone is getting delivered from a demon, they have to be immediately filled up with Jesus. Otherwise, the devil will find the place empty and come back sevenfold (see Matthew 12:43–45).

In church circles, this is known as deliverance. The church has taken so many opportunities to free people from demons and demonic activity through simple deliverance in Jesus without them knowing Jesus was the one delivering them. This is why spiritual cleansing is always accompanied by "redefinement," which is salvation. It's becoming a new creation and getting a new identity. When we offer this, seekers know that they will leave a different person if they ask to have a redefinement experience.

Almost everyone we've seen have a spiritual encounter with the Spirit of Truth (the Holy Spirit) began to shake under the power of God and speak in tongues. These are people who did not have any understanding of the Bible at all, yet when the Holy Spirit would come on them, they would intensely feel His presence. As they began to speak in a new language, we knew they were going to be a new creation as well. It is absolutely amazing.

We have many further examples of fun ways to connect with people. Here are a few other items on our menu board for outreach. All of these tools and this language can be incorporated on outreach events or in regular interactions with seekers in your life.

HEART TRANSFORMATION

Ask if you may put your hand on their heart and speak life words to it. Prophetically remove the callused places and barbed wire around their hearts that keep them from feeling. Ask for their heart to be transformed. Ask that the Spirit of Truth would saturate their heart to open them up to new beginnings. Identify with pain they may share with you, especially if you have gone through something similar. Find common ground. We've all been hurt, so it's not hard. *Never play Holy Ghost Junior* by correcting people. That's not our job. Allow the love and healing balm to flow out of you. God will give you compassion.

MEET THE SPIRIT OF TRUTH

I ask everyone who walks into the Freedom Lounge, "Do you want to have an encounter with the Spirit of Truth?" After all, who doesn't, right? This is so simple and so fun! We ask them to put their hands out and then we ask the Spirit of Truth to come. The Holy Spirit shows up, rocking them to their core,

NEW LANGUAGE TO REACH THE SEEKERS

and when He does, they tip their heads back, speaking in tongues, and shake uncontrollably. Tears fill their eyes and roll down their face. It is always radical.

When I think about Burning Man as an event geared toward radical self-expression, I have noticed that when you get the Holy Spirit into a place of openness, He is radically self-expressive!

We had to unlearn a lot of our behavior because God wants to reach these seekers the way they *can* be reached, not the way we *want* to reach them. After an encounter, most people would ask, "What just happened to me?" More often than not, most would say something like this:

"I feel like my lungs were just opened."

"I feel like the fog is off of my mind."

"I feel like my eyes are open, the sky is blue, and the grass is green."

"I feel like I received something new. Something happened to me."

"I do not feel the same anymore."

I knew they had just had an encounter, an Organic Spiritual Alignment, with God the Father, the One who loves them. He is radical and will do anything to get their attention.

One of my favorite stories is when a man came through the tent wearing occult-like jewelry and almost no clothing. He listened to the drums for a while and joined in for a short time. He walked from booth to booth until someone showed him the menu board. He took one look at Original Root Recovery and was in. This guy was buzzing with anticipation as I asked,

"Do you want an encounter with the Spirit of Truth?" He said yes, of course. I told him to hold out his hands like he was being given a gift.

I'm not kidding. A jolt of Holy Spirit power shot through my hands into his and he jumped—literally jumped off the ground. Without a word to me, he walked up to every person in the Freedom Lounge and said, "The Spirit of Truth is Jesus Christ. Did you know the Spirit of Truth is Jesus? Jesus is the Spirit of Truth." He came back a few more times after that. The encounter changed his life, and ours, forever.

I asked for his name, and he said, "Abraham." God sent Abraham into our tent and changed him instantly by an encounter with the Holy Spirit who revealed Himself to this man as Jesus. What a powerful revelation from this God encounter.

FROM THEIR OWN MOUTHS

The Freedom Lounge and our team had gotten so popular that Burning Man staff contacted us and asked where we would like our camp placed. This was because they heard testimonies like this:

"My name is Kool-Aid or Chris, depending on your mood. That was the most incredible, pure, and deeply cleansing experience of my entire life. I am a Reiki Master. I have gone to school for these types of things, and nothing I have ever experienced in my life compares to what I just had. It was peace. It was easy. It was pure, clean, and left me feeling like whatever happened there is still going to take place over the

NEW LANGUAGE TO REACH THE SEEKERS

next couple days. I just kind of have to readjust to whatever the hell I am right now. This is the moment I have been looking for since I got on the plane. So, thank you, all of you. This has been a beautiful experience. Thank you so much."

The young man named Chris, who works in the tech industry, got drunk in the Spirit in our tent. It was a powerful encounter with God, and when it was over, Chris had no idea where or in what direction he needed to go. He literally could not find his tent. We had to guide him until his friends came to help. Now he comes every year and brings people to see us. God is so patient with His friends, and we've learned to be patient too.

A woman who attended a spiritual alignment session told us this:

> I have this reoccurring dream that I can breathe underwater. And there is a moment of discovery when I know that I'm underwater and I'm swimming, and I know that I don't have to surface because I know I can breathe. I never knew what it meant, but the lady who interpreted my dream said the Spirit is around me. The water is the Spirit, and I can breathe it in. The Spirit calls me his daughter and there is a big white rose in the middle of me, and I plant flowers as I walk and bring joy to everybody. That's pretty cool.

This girl never knew what her dream meant until I told her the water is the Spirit of Truth all around her. She started to cry as I shared the meaning of her dream, one that she'd had "for years and years and years." I believe the dream interpretation opened a door for a conversation between God and His beloved friend, who just needed to breathe Him in and see the purity of what He had planted within her.

One of our team members was our "barker." A barker has the job of stopping people who pass by and asking them if they want to visit our camp. His name was Gambit and he did card tricks. The Burners called it "magic," but we knew better. Gambit would draw people over and connect with them through his card tricks, then invite them into our tent where we would "pull the gold out of them." He would do his card trick, and when the people were in awe, he would say things like, "If you think this is amazing, you should go inside the tent. Our team will show you the gold that is really inside you and reveal the fresh identity about yourself."

Inside our tent we looked inside each person for all the "gold," also known as the gifts, identity, and purpose placed there by God. Through prayer, intercession, and the intervention of the Holy Spirit, we brought it to the surface and showed them how valuable they truly were. In the process, we would break down a bunch of junk—lies, hurts, and bad habits—that had been blocking them from their destiny. Then we would speak life over them before telling them they are free to go. Most of them choose not to go. Instead, they stick around in the Holy Spirit's atmosphere because for the first time in a long time, they feel clean. In those moments, their whole lives are being redefined by Jesus.

CHAPTER 8

THERE'S NO HURT LIKE CHURCH HURT

The spiritual hunger of the Burners is off the charts, often because so many of them are from the church. We frequently meet pastor's kids, worship leaders, ministry leaders, and pastors who left because they were misunderstood and mistreated. It was made clear they did not fit in with the stained-glass crowd.

God cannot be contained in a box. Neither can the artists, free thinkers, and creatives. The church has not really made a place for them to express their creativity. Consequently, many of the people we meet have been turned off by the church simply for not being allowed to be who they were created to be.

They love and connect with the Lord in different ways than we do. The Western church at large has not achieved an understanding of its creatives and artisans. Because of this, the artists are pushed aside and eventually go where they have the freedom to connect with others who also have an artistic nature. When this happens, they typically reject the idea of Jesus, who was terribly misrepresented by their church, in exchange for the sense of belonging in a community.

Community involvement and relationship is woven into the very fabric of our existence. God put it there, but people have let each other down. That disappointment drives us toward whoever will accept us as we are. Let's face it: the church can be the most judgmental place of all, even though it isn't supposed to be.

The enemy has done a great job of exchanging job descriptions with "Jesus." In doing so, he shifts blame onto Jesus for the very things the devil is actually doing himself, like breaking community and stripping us of our identities. God is chasing hard after those He loves unconditionally. As we realize the condition of our current culture, we now have an opportunity and an invitation—almost a mandate—to redefine Jesus to a generation that thinks He is something other than Love in its purest form.

A PASTOR IS STILL A PASTOR ACCORDING TO GOD

It was "Tutu Tuesday," so Steven came to the Freedom Lounge wearing nothing but a pink tutu. I know this because a member of my team told me not to look down. He was a burly guy with the beard to match and looked like a truck driver. He stood before me holding another man's hand. We asked him if he would like to have an encounter with the Spirit of Truth. A man of few words, Steven answered simply, "Yes."

He extended his arms with the palms of his hands up and said, "Spirit of Truth, come." Steven soon started to cry. He was a thick, muscular guy and just began sobbing and sobbing. The Spirit of God had suddenly come over him in a very tangible way. I could feel the Spirit all over him. He said to me, "I know what this is."

I asked, "What is it?"

Steven said, "It is the Holy Spirit."

"Yes, it is," I replied.

When he was finally able to speak, Steven said, "I was a pastor. My wife left me for another man. I had no idea anything was going on. My denomination replaced me with another pastor in our church and kicked me out. They fired me although I had done nothing wrong. I've been so deeply hurt and confused that I was losing hope in not only my own identity, but also in God."

The betrayal seeped through his voice. His pain was palpable. I told him how sorry I was about his situation and that it was not God's plan for him. The words flowed freely as the Holy Spirit spoke through me to Steven: "God did not do this to you. The gifts and callings of God are irrevocable, and God has not changed the calling He has placed on your life. He has plans for you and a purpose. In fact, God has a new restart for you. His will and plan is to restore you and open doors for you to be the person He has called you to be on this earth. He always makes a way where there seems to be no way. When your heart breaks, His heart breaks, but you already know this."

I told him, "You were called, saved, and anointed for service in the Kingdom of God. Just because it did not work out and something really awful happened to you does not discredit or cancel out God's plan for you."

He said he wanted to get back with God. I let him know he was welcome to stay with us all week long if he needed to. I told him we would feed him, take care of him, and bring him back into a place where he could be restored into the call and the purpose of God in his life. I let him know we had people who had extra clothes if or when he needed them. If he was ready, we wanted to help him get back into restoration with God.

He came back that day clothed and brought all of his belongings with him. Romans 8:28 shows us that God truly works all things for our good when we love Him and are called according to His purpose.

The Lord loves people. He will chase them down with His love. He is not moved or threatened by anything they have gotten themselves into. There is no measure to the depth of His love, no limit to the lengths He will go to reach one person and bring them into their original purpose. The more I saw God chase after people at Burning Man and other events—the more I saw His crazy, unconditional love and His non-condemning way of reaching people who lived all kinds of lifestyles—the more I loved Him myself. He is *the* fantastic life-giver.

CHAPTER 9

THE HEART OF THE SEEKER GENERATION

We are living in a day and time that is unprecedented in so many ways. As a pastor friend of mine likes to say, "Never have we lived in a day when you can get so messed up so fast." There's an acceleration of technology, communications, wealth, travel, and information. With it comes an acceleration of evil because the time is short.

All of our lives have been shaped by bad circumstances, abuse, times of being undervalued, and others. Unless we ask to listen, we will never know the stories of the people around us.

Creatives are often traumatized by their life journey. They think artistically. They express themselves from the core of who they truly are. Creatives are absolutely brilliant. They have this incredible ability to see beyond the obvious and look into the depth of things. Because of their adept ability to view the world in colorful and abstract ways, they were often made fun of and mocked for "not fitting the mold" in their formative years.

Identify them according to the positive perception of who *they* think they are and build a bridge to speak life. You must cancel anything that would keep them from fulfilling their destiny. Value what they value, even if it's not what we value. Listen instead of talking. Once a friendship is established, God will show you their heart, and healing words will come out of your mouth and into their spirit.

Over the years, we have learned that so many people do not trust. There have been too many harsh messages and passed judgments from the church to those who are hurting and broken and nowhere near enough about God's love for them. While the harsh truths of the Bible are important, we have to model the way Jesus reached the people He called His friends. For starters, if you have harsh dialogue with a person you don't have a relationship with and call them out by their sin instead of who they really are, you will only push them further away from God. We have seen this time and time again.

God always looks at the heart, not at outward appearance. We do not know their story or what they have been through. There is no way of knowing what words have been spoken to them, how they have been neglected, or when their innocence was stolen from them. If we, the church, only deliver harsh messages and refuse to look at people through God's eyes of love, we drive them further away to wander around and explore other things. They will plug in where they find community, friendship, and acceptance. If we are not the source of community, the world will be!

It is extremely important that we learn to do things God's way. John 3:17 clearly tells us that God did not send Jesus into the world to condemn the world. The world was already condemned. God sent Jesus to a world that was broken, hurting, angry, and deceived. If we are going to bring people into freedom from their trauma, from their past and their pain, and give them a whole new identity, we have got to do things very differently.

There is a compelling factor that God gives us when we are reaching the God-hardened, Godless, and God-confused. He allowed me to see three young men who visited our camp through His eyes. All three of them had been sexually abused as children. They felt dirty. They felt separated. They felt trashed, and they didn't like themselves at all. They had found each other and formed a community together based on their similar stories and backgrounds. Their friendships were built on a trauma bond. The Lord wanted to set them free, but first there had to be a demonstration of the unconditional love of God in their lives before they would even allow us to talk with them on any level about Him.

One of the men spoke up and said they had gone to church during the tender time of their identity-searching process and were scolded by the people in leadership for their lifestyle. There was no consideration of what they had walked through.

They had found no listening ear and definitely no loving heart toward them.

We have to remember that love always, *always* transforms its object. Roman 2:4 tells us that the kindness of God leads people to repentance. We are not Holy Ghost Junior. The Holy Spirit convicts of sin when the love of God has been demonstrated to a person who is living a life contrary to how God designed them to live. Otherwise, we're all on the chopping block. Psalm 130:3 poses the question, "If You, Lord, should mark iniquities, O Lord, who could stand?"

We must have compassion and love in our hearts. Compassion, through the power of the Holy Spirit, is the very fuel that propelled Jesus to tirelessly go about healing all who were oppressed of the devil. First Corinthians 13 tells us that without love and compassion, we are nothing more than sounding brass or a clanging cymbal. That's why it's so important for us to learn how to love.

We need to learn how to listen to hear and understand instead of listening to respond. We have to learn how God wants us to reach His friends. Psalm 34:18 says God is very near "to those who have a broken heart," and Psalm 46:1 says He is "a very present help in trouble."

We live in a world where people are broken, hurting, and don't trust others because of their past life experiences. Words don't have value unless there is a trust bridge between people first. Old methods of outreach and telling strangers about Jesus on the streets just don't work like they did in the 1970s. We've often found that saying the name "Jesus" only creates an argument. The very people we were trying to reach felt shame and condemnation, even though that was never the intent of the conversation.

God told me He wanted me to be teachable to new ways, new language, new ideas, creative expressions, and how to communicate Him to a world who sees Him much differently than I do. In this chapter, we will discover some of the creative ways God had us reach into "God-hardened" hearts with a message of hope.

FOUR DOGS, TWO GIRLS, AND A MESSAGE

At a coffee shop a while back, I noticed a young woman sitting outside with three rescue dogs by her side. She was just enjoying some coffee and the dogs seemed friendly, so I approached her and asked if I could pet her dogs. She was more than welcoming to me and began telling me all about her dogs and how she ended up with each of them.

"This one was abused, this one was left on the side of the road, and this one was given to me by a friend who was moving and didn't want to deal with hassle," she told me. At that moment, I got a total picture of her life. She was a single girl with huge trust issues.

She asked me if I wanted to join her at her table, and I gladly accepted the offer. I thanked her for her willingness to care for these rescue dogs and explained that it takes a special kind of person to do something like that. Her arms had big scars all over them. The scars also appeared above her knees and on her chest. I asked her what had happened to her and she explained that it was "skin art," like a tattoo, except this practice was done with a scalpel and no anesthetic.

I tried to keep a very unemotional face as I asked her to explain the significance of this art style. She told me that a person actually pays to have this done, and the biggest one cost her about $250. She explained that it's a way to release inner pain and regain control over things that she had been subject to growing up. She told me the artist takes a scalpel and cuts into the skin about one-eighth of an inch deep, depending on the design. The artist then takes hemostats and pulls the cut skin from her body while she presses the wound with gauze to help stop the bleeding.

As the healing of the wound starts, it produces a scar in a certain pattern to serve as a sign that the painful memory didn't control her anymore. I was completely engaged in her conversation, listening to every word as God downloaded His wisdom on how to proceed with this new information.

While she continued to speak, I became more aware of what God was wanting me to know. He revealed to me that each of the dogs represented her life. She had been abused by members of her family since she was a little girl, she was then left on her own when she was twelve years old. Her grandmother took her in and gave her shelter, but she felt like she was an inconvenience to her and not a desire.

Then I told her that I was an "inner healer" and work in the "healing arts." The language began to pour out of my mouth, and I found myself using the word *art* in my description of myself because of how much she valued art. I felt my hand get hot and I asked if I could put my hand on the scar on her chest and trace the scar with my hand. She agreed and I felt God's healing power flowing into her, and so did she. I told her that I am a "follower of Jesus" as my spiritual life and journey, and that Jesus knows about scars. I said, "He has scars on His body, too, and He not only identifies with your pain, but is present to heal it and take it from you because of His love for you."

She was now intrigued by my value system of life. I asked if she would be open for me to do some healing on her to clear up any unsettled issues in her life. I asked if she would allow me to ask the Creator to connect her in the Spirit realm and find the "Way, the Truth, and the Life." She gladly accepted my invitation.

I clasped her hand and asked the "Light" to shine on her and give her an encounter with the "Designer" of her life. She closed her eyes and the Holy Spirit took over. I could feel His presence surrounding us as her pain turned into unexplained joy. In John 6:44, Jesus says, "No one can come to Me unless the Father who sent Me draws him." The Lord was drawing this girl closer to him.

She asked me what she was feeling, and I then had the opportunity to share with her about the person of Jesus and His vast love of her. This was not a short conversation. She was so overjoyed to understand something that day that would begin a new life for her. I realized that she was in a process of understanding of Jesus, so I didn't press any further that day, but I ended up seeing her a couple more times. She did indeed ask Jesus to become the Lord of her life. We don't always have to seal the deal right away. God knows where everyone is in their process of coming to Him, so we just need to follow his direction.

Another time, we were hosting an outreach in New Orleans at a bar/restaurant named "Saints and Sinners." The owner of the bar was a new Christian and wanted to use the space for people to meet Jesus. He had an assistant manager who was not at all happy about this decision. Body language told us much—her "walled-off" posture was speaking loud and clear—but she had a dog. We had created an outreach at this venue, and we had small groups around small bar tables to minister to people who wanted an "encounter with the Spirit of Truth."

The assistant manager was watching people go up and down the stairs all evening. She approached one of the team members and asked them to ask me if I "read dogs." This was new for me. I remembered that Psalm 150:6 says, "let everything that has breath praise the Lord," so I said, "Of course I do!" I wondered what I had gotten myself into, but God reminded me of the woman who had rescued three dogs with similar circumstances as her. I approached the assistant manager's dog with the same understanding.

The dog was about six years old, was in a harness, was not aggressive, and was pretty well-behaved. As I pet the dog, I asked God what to say, as I knew whatever was said to the dog would sink into its owner. Another man on the team, who had a strong prophetic gift, was there to help me "read the dog."

THE HEART OF THE SEEKER GENERATION

He was tracking with the Holy Spirit and me, so we began to call out positive qualities about the faithfulness of this dog, his protective instincts, his ability to spot danger from a distance, and his pathway that would lead him to a healed new life. We spoke a healing balm over his wounded heart and trauma places. We asked for his Creator to open him up to being loved again. My team member and I continued down this road of destiny built on words, and when I looked up, the owner was crying and hugging her dog. She thanked us over and over again and again for reading the dog.

LAS VEGAS ENTERTAINER AND HIS FRIENDS

I had the privilege of ministering to a young performer from Las Vegas who came to the Freedom Lounge to have an encounter with the Spirit of Truth. He was a relatively well-known performer in Vegas, but at Burning Man, everyone is considered to be on the same level. He wanted to have an Organic Spiritual Alignment, so I took his hands and told him to ask for the Spirit of Truth to come—and He did.

I immediately had words of knowledge for him and knew that he was a worshiper. I was standing about six feet away from him, and as I pointed at him, power came out of my finger. He was knocked backwards over his chair as a voice roared out of me, saying, "You are a worshiper! You are called to worship! That is what God has created you for!"

Until that time, I had never said words like that at our theme camp. We are very careful about using the words *God* or *Jesus* because of the misunderstandings of those who are seeking.

They must encounter Him before they will see who God really is.

When he fell back over the chair, he lay on the ground crying and weeping as he curled up in a ball. It was evident the Creator was all over him. This young man, living openly in a bisexual lifestyle, was in our theme camp for about two and a half hours having an encounter with the Holy Spirit. Later, I found out that his grandparents were pastors. I knew that God was doing a deep work in him.

After some time had passed, my daughter and I went to Las Vegas and we gave him a call. He told us he wanted to take us somewhere, so of course we obliged. He took us to the lobby of a hotel where there was no gaming (which is strange for Vegas). All of the paintings on the wall were pictures of people with no faces, which spoke volumes to me. The paintings described the community that he lived in and was connected to. He took us around the corner to the bar, where we met thirty to forty young homosexual men. Their ages ranged from roughly eighteen years old to maybe thirty-five years old. These were his friends, and one of them had a birthday.

I said, "This is incredible! I have a birthday gift for you!" For the next five hours, I sat there giving prophetic words, interpreting dreams, and loving on those young people with God's unconditional love. We tried to leave a couple of times, but they begged me to stay a little longer. I asked the bartender for some water, and he gave me a bottle labeled "Liquid Salvation." It was such a cool experience. We didn't leave until 2:30 in the morning.

After this man took us back to our hotel, God spoke to

me and said, "These are my friends. The young man that you prayed for and spoke prophetically to at Burning Man is my friend. If you will love my friends, I will introduce them to you. What you just experienced is my heart for people who don't know me yet. You loved the one I sent you, and he introduced you to his friends. Although you weren't able to tell them about me, my love was able to pour through you to them. I will not let them forget that."

People are in a process of coming to Jesus and understanding that they can have new life in Him. They are wading through their own condemnation and do not feel that they deserve grace. They are in process, and anytime God uses us to touch one of His friends, God will make sure that they never forget it. He will bring it to mind for them time and time again.

When I'm interpreting dreams in an outreach setting, I always ask God to highlight people to me so that I know who I need to meet. As I walked through the front door, I noticed two women sitting on a couch. God strongly highlighted one of the women on the couch. Then I noticed that her heart looked like it had three strands of barbed wire around it. As I got closer, she could tell that I was looking at her. I introduced myself and said, "I know it sounds awkward, but sometimes I see things about people—and I can see your heart. It looks as if you have three strands of barbed wire on your heart, and I don't think you're able to feel because it's being strangled."

She was very open to hearing what I saw and thought about her. I said, "I am a heart healer, and if you wouldn't mind, I want to just remove the three strands." She said it was okay and questioned how one would do that. I took my hand and motioned as if I were pulling three strands of barbed wire off of her heart. Then I asked her if I could put my hand on her heart. She allowed it. When I touched her, I asked for healing to begin to flow into her heart and to allow her to feel again. I asked that she'd be able to breathe again and for her heart to come back to life.

What I was seeing prophetically, she was experiencing physically. I said to her, "I believe this is generational and it started with your mother's mother. I think your grandmother had an experience with a man that was not good, which created in her a man-hating spirit. It trickled down from your grandmother to your mom, and now to you." She told me I was right. Without using words, I asked God to heal her wounded heart and allow her to feel His presence. I did this without words because she was feeling His presence, and my words at that moment would have gotten in the way of her encounter.

As Christians, we must relearn how to love others. The church has done well enough at teaching people how to judge. When will we spend more time learning how we will love others?

In the early 1990s, I had an emotional breakdown after pastoring churches. God showed me how little I loved what He loves and how I was operating in ways and thoughts that were not His. He started me on a journey to understand his unconditional love for people, for myself, and for His church. His arms are constantly open to the broken, regardless of what condition they're in. I asked Him to teach me His ways, how to love, and how He sees the people that need to be reached. I asked Him to show me how He loves me so that I could love myself.

God began to teach me about His unconditional love. I began to understand that God is an unconditional Lover regardless of how people got into the situations they're in. I began to develop a great love for people who lived a completely different life than me. I could literally feel my heart change when I knew I was going to have an encounter with someone. I knew that it wasn't my heart beating, but God's heart beating in me. I began to have compassion that wasn't my own. I didn't possess that kind of compassion or love in my normal body, heart, or mind. It was a supernatural love because Jesus lives inside me. I understood for a brief moment what it felt like to partake of a divine nature.

LETTING GOD TAKE OVER

My whole life is outreach. My desire is to see people come to the knowledge of Jesus, the Spirit and the Truth. This burns inside me all the time. I can remember on the moments on outreach when my heart would start to beat differently, which indicated that I was getting ready to have an encounter that God had set up. He had ordered my steps ahead of me.

It gave me great confidence because I knew that if my steps are ordered by Him, and I'm getting ready to have an encounter with someone that He loves, then I would also have His words, His heart, and His love inside me for the encounter they needed. I could feel the angelic help surrounding me during that time, and I would hear things in my ear that I knew were from angels. I have even been told my eyes change and light comes out of them during some encounters. God always gives me specific words of knowledge for the person I am talking to. I don't consider myself to be highly gifted, but when the Holy Spirit is on me and I'm having a divine appointment, I become highly gifted. When I step out to reach someone, I fervently experience the Holy Spirit inside me. This is what happens when we seek out God's heart and give him full control over our lives and actions.

We were in New York, at Times Square, when I met a young man who was a street performer. He was on a break, and I asked if I could interpret a dream for him. He said he had just had one the night before. It has become more and more typical that people will have a dream the night before I end up speaking to them. The young man told me a dream about his father who had passed away. In the dream, he said his father lay on his bed and tickled him. He told me he had an incredible relationship with his father and that he really missed him.

I knew that this dream brought him great joy, and that his dream father represented both his earthly father and his heavenly Father. He was being comforted and loved by God the Creator. The young man did not like my answer because he did not believe that God was male. As I was listening to him, he began to argue with me about my interpretation.

I began asking God at the same time, "What would you

like me to say to him?" I could feel the Holy Spirit on me, and I knew He would give me an answer for this young man. As I was listening to God to get an answer for him, my eyes begin to change. Light came out of my eyes, and it stopped him in the middle of his sentence.

He got very close to my face and said, "Who is that in you looking back at me?" I replied, "It's God the Father, the one that we're talking about. Your earthly father is not here anymore, and your earthly father loved you very much, but God your Father is still here and in your life. He is watching you and will never leave you. He will always be your source of strength if you will let Him."

That was the first time I can remember having that kind of experience. However, it is pretty common now that God moves through me in these ways. He communicates with me and gives me such insight that my eyes will actually change color and light will come out from them. When that happens, the people that I'm talking to become spellbound. This supernatural demonstration from heaven is confirmation that what I am saying is true.

I think we often get hung up and limit ourselves on what we think we can do, when God is so much bigger. He has got so much more of Himself that He wants to reveal in ways we've never seen before—ways we could never imagine. I encourage you to ask God to take over your actions and presence and give you downloads of the supernatural. God will work in so many different ways. He loves to surprise us.

ENTERING PORN CONVENTIONS

When the Lord asked me if I wanted to meet His friends, He didn't disappoint! Although I hadn't really thought about what that meant when I answered, "Your friends will be my friends, Jesus," I quickly found out He had friends everywhere. I really mean everywhere. While at Burning Man, we found many of the broken and hurting people we met were from the pornography industry. We met porn stars and porn addicts, yes, but also producers, directors, camera crew, and editors—creatives who worked on the less acceptable side of the film realm. I had no history with the porn industry or what went on at their conventions, but I felt it couldn't get much worse than what we saw at Burning Man.

Boy, was I wrong.

There were eight of us on the team, with one of our members being an actual survivor of sexual abuse. Because of her past personal involvement with the industry, she understood its blatant Sodom-and-Gomorrah-type of perversion. The convention had the same deviant atmosphere she had witnessed before, growing like a cancer and especially pursuing our young people.

I, on the other hand, am a pastor and mother of two daughters. As I got my badge and walked toward the entrance, I kept thinking, *What's a nice mom like you doing in a place like this?* Amidst the initial shock of the pure sexual hype and debauchery of it all, I felt as if all the air in my lungs had been forced out of me. I couldn't breathe and it was evident why.

On the wall behind each vendor's booth played

compromising videos of young girls. Most looked barely eighteen, if that. The music boomed deafeningly, and I felt like I had stepped into the pit of hell. I could feel myself start to shut down in every way as I continued to lead my team inside. I was choking on the fear, shame, and isolation I saw in the faces around me, especially the actresses. They were smiling but also not, teasing yet testing each person who came to their booth for any tiny shred of real compassion or decency. Tears streamed down my face as I walked the aisle of the convention center, trying not to look to the right or left. It was all so hopeless.

I stopped for a split second and asked God, "What do I do?"

He replied, "I've already seen it. You're seated with me in heavenly places, so keep the peace I give you. I have a plan." He went on to tell me that He saw everything that was happening without the lewdness. It wasn't long before I was looking through His eyes and the nudity started to fade. I started to see beyond the fake smiles and false bravado. I started to see the heart and who these people really were to the One who made them.

Instantly, I calmed down. All my outreach efforts and my Burning Man experience had taught me to look at the heart and not the outward appearance—to look for the gold in others no matter how far gone they seemed to be.

NOTHING SHOCKS GOD

The stories of the walking wounded here were just horrible. Some of the young girls and boys had been abused since they were little. They were shattered and broken, and they felt like they had nowhere else to go. Here, they said, they fit in. They'd formed a pack of broken people who understood one another's pain. A picture of Sid's toys from the movie *Toy Story* flashed through my head. They were all disfigured on the inside and did not look like what they were created for.

We eventually passed by a booth that had a pink cross on it. I stopped and the girl from behind the table suddenly grabbed my arm, saying, "I'm going to pray for you." I was shocked and pleasantly surprised. Her name was Shelley Lubben. She founded the Pink Cross Foundation, which rescues girls from the porn industry, after she had left the industry and encountered Jesus. I don't even remember what she said in her prayer, but I instantly felt peace. My mind cleared and I knew God had direction for our team on this battleground. From that moment on, I navigated throughout the convention center, looking for the people God had sent us in there to reach. It was both an outreach and a training ground for me.

At these conventions, talent scouts, pimps, filmmakers, agents, and sex toy vendors are spread out all over the convention room floor. Like the Academy Awards, the young actresses are nominated for different awards based on their sex acts—the more graphic or unusual, the higher the "esteem" of the award.

Our team decided to turn this outreach into a fact-finding mission to see how people actually decided to join such a destructive industry. While it took some digging and lots of patience, the majority of young girls admitted they had been sexually abused since they were young, usually by a family member, friend of the family, neighbor, or babysitter. In short, the people they trusted could not be trusted. One young girl told us she was the "family sex toy" and fake-laughed at the statement. Behind her bravado lay a shattered life of stolen innocence and false identity. Several girls told us they joined the industry because a friend was involved in it and "the money was good."

We continued our journey down the rabbit hole of deviancy when it dawned on me that the porn industry is its own planet. The abuse and sickness had crept into their minds so deeply that this lifestyle seemed normal to them. Most girls we talked to did not see anything wrong with it, even though their bodies were in constant pain from the physical abuse and mental strife. Why? They felt they deserved it.

As the day went on, I could hear God's heart saying, "I want these people and I want them bad. Remember, they are my friends—all of them." I was wrestling with my own emotions. Somewhere between heartbreak at this hideous deception and looking to Jesus for His instruction and love, my perception changed. Judgment and condemnation were not even on my radar, just an open-armed and heartfelt response to go after the ones who desperately needed to find the Way.

CHAPTER 10

GOD'S HEART FOR THE SEEKERS

Attending the porn convention for the first time was definitely a life-changing experience. I knew my paradigms had been forever shifted by the heartbreak I saw behind the costumes, makeup, and obligatory come-ons the girls gave to those passing by their booth. If an investor picked them up for a role, it meant less abuse and a few more months of "stability."

These girls were captives, and so were those pimping them out, financing the movies, and directing them. The entire industry is captive to the dark agenda of lies and deception. I had a deep sense of the kind, empathetic heart of God. I imagined how He must have felt when He, moved by compassion, healed everyone who came to Him. Everyone. We read about it in Matthew 9:35–35:

Then Jesus went about all the cities and villages, teaching in their synagogues, preaching the gospel of the kingdom, and healing every sickness and every disease among the people. But when He saw the multitudes, He was moved with compassion for them, because they were weary and scattered, like sheep having no shepherd.

I caught a glimpse of His overwhelming desire to grab people and bring them out of this false, destructive world, into a new life He had for them—the new life waiting on the other side of their decision to let Him in. My spirit welled up with that same desire as if the Lord were pouring it into me from a giant waterfall.

Being a mom, I carried the ability to minister from a mother's heart. I wanted to sit with these young girls and hear their stories, comfort their cries, and figure out how I could give them good direction and wise counsel for the days ahead. I used dreams and interpretation as a conversation starter, and they were very open to it. Despite the hell of their daily lives, despite their distance from God, I knew He was still speaking to them.

OUR INVITATION TO BE ON PLAYBOY RADIO

While on outreach to our first porn convention, our team saw many disturbing display booths from companies within the industry. One of the companies had a fascination with death. These types of companies are called "fetish" companies. They are designed to create a feeling of shock and awe of demonic enticement to lower the bar of seductive experiences.

GOD'S HEART FOR THE SEEKERS

I had to keep my focus on Jesus so I would stay in His peace in the midst of this hideous display. There is no room for knee-jerk responses here, so we had to learn to respond instead of reacting.

I had an "investor" badge on and people willingly talked to me, probably because they thought there might be some financial investment from me for their companies.

This is the world we live in that the church doesn't see.

As I moved on throughout the convention, I was standing in front of a table of people with headphones on. They were broadcasting on a syndicate station and reaching a very wide audience. I was still processing how to reach the people in this arena and waiting for one of my team members to connect with me at this location because we had been separated. As I stood there, a man approached me from the Playboy radio table and asked me if I wanted to be on the radio to take live sex call-ins.

I looked around and behind me, thinking he was talking to someone else. I mean, I'm a mom, dressed very much like a mom. I seemed to be the least likely person someone would approach with that question. "Are you asking me?" I said.

"Yes, we want you to put the headphones on and be on the radio with us to take calls and answer questions about sex." I started laughing in his face. He wasn't laughing. He was serious.

Without thinking, I said to him, "Well, I don't do *that*, but I do dream interpretations." He became even more interested and told me how fascinating that would be for callers to be able to get my input on their sex dreams over the radio.

I thought for a minute (again, no knee-jerk responses) and said, "Well, give me your card and I'll ask the Boss and see what He says about my participation in doing a show with you."

He then said, "This is crazy, because last night I had a vivid dream about being on a train and then changing trains to go in the opposite direction."

I told him, "You are in transition and you are changing tracks, having reached the end of this season you are in. You're now going to be heading out of this porn arena and getting on track with your *real* purpose and destiny. It will be something you were meant for and not what you have settled for."

He responded with elation. He had been planning on leaving the industry and wanted to get his life "on track" again. I didn't end up going on the radio since it was my first time in that type of arena, but I still walked away in awe of how the young man came to ask me of all people to be on the show.

This was one of the many instances when God gave a person a dream the night before they ran into me or one of our team members on outreach. We have God's answer for them at that time as we interpret their dream for them.

DREAMS OPEN DOORS

Through dream interpretation, I knew I had something that could benefit the lives of the people at the porn convention. Whenever I mentioned dream interpretation, all their walls of resistance suddenly faded out of existence. They told me beautiful dreams of purpose and destiny they'd had as young kids. Some had experienced self-impacting scary dreams,

GOD'S HEART FOR THE SEEKERS

which were usually about being chased or about loved ones who had died. Fear had crept into their lives through these nightmares and had manifested in so many ways.

Before I go any further, let me say this: no little girl ever woke up one day and said, "I want to take off all my clothes and have sex with strangers in front of a camera." Not one. Every little girl has dreams of family, success, belonging, purpose, and joy. So many of our sons and daughters have found those dreams cut off or ripped out because of abandonment or abuse. Almost all of those in the porn industry have been abused, most of them by the very people who were supposed to protect them. They are broken and lost, but God speaks to them often and vividly through dreams. He is so kind and gentle. He wants to get their attention without shame or blame.

Dreams are vast and the number of dreamers is inexhaustible. Literally everybody dreams. I call dreams a "pass key," similar to the key that hotel workers carry to enter any room. I have rarely been turned down when I ask people if they would like to have a dream interpreted.

When they tell me their dreams, they are giving me a glimpse into their lives. I have now interpreted thousands of dreams all over the world. God asked me to learn to interpret dreams because it is His secret language for giving people a message regardless of whether they believe in Him. The more time I've invested in learning to interpret dreams, the more skilled I have become.

There are now times when a person will begin to tell me a dream and I will be able to finish it for them. It is like a Daniel moment, where God tells me the dream as they are telling me the dream. Now that gets someone's attention! People are so encouraged and blessed when we take time to listen to them and let them be heard.

Dream interpretation is based on a value system. You value someone so much that you allow them to share their heart with you. We have learned to listen to hear, rather than listen to respond. Dream interpretation is one of my favorite ways of communicating with Jesus' friends. It builds a bridge. You don't need to interpret dreams for God to work through you, but our teams have found it to be one of the most effective outreach tools of this day and age.

When anyone gives out prophetic words, even in treasure hunting, people have to decide whether they want to hear a word from a stranger. People sometimes get freaked out and don't really receive the good word they are hearing because they think it is too good to be true. However, dream interpretation only happens when the person we are talking to shares something and thus, lowers the bridge of connection themselves.

Another major key to reaching into the hearts of today's seekers, especially those in the porn industry, is listening well. When we emphatically listen with our hearts, we shove all of our thoughts out of our heads and become available as a person lowers a gateway into their heart. Trust is formed and we are able to communicate truth, love, and wisdom in a pure way as God gives us language to share His purpose in "un-churchy" language.

We must always remember that those caught up in

sexual perversion have been turned off by church. They have a warped perception of Jesus and want no part in a religious box that suffocates their creativity and individuality.

As we make our way out to the highways and hedges in this great harvest, let's remember that it is God's love that compels and His Spirit that guides. When we learn to follow the leading of the Holy Spirit and not our learned techniques, God will introduce us to His friends. He is not condemning or judgmental. It is not our job to correct people. It is our mandate to love them.

PASTOR'S DAUGHTER AT PORN CONVENTION

We are looking for the gold in others, no matter who they are or what they do. People make choices and decisions to go into different arenas based on their friends, their culture, and their upbringing. But there is always a divine purpose for the way we are meant to live. So it is important to look for what God wants us to do.

When we go into a place where much sin abounds, we need grace to abound even more (see Romans 5:20). It is easy to get overwhelmed by what you see and hear. You must look where God looks, on their hearts. God told me a few years back when we started doing this, "If you will put your finger on the pulse of culture, I will bring you the encounters." We know our steps are ordered by Him. He set this whole thing up.

One time at a porn convention, a young woman volunteered personal information and told us she was from a pastor's family. I thought she said a Baptist family, but she corrected me and said, "No, a pastor's family." My response was, "Oh, you're a PK," which is short for preacher's or pastor's kid. Then she knew she was busted.

I told her, "The unconditional love of God doesn't fail. He's never left you. He's never going to leave you, and He loves you even in the choices you make. His calling on your life and His pathway for you is still there. You just have to get back on track." She broke down when I talked to her about the unconditional love that does not fail. I told her, "I know there are greater things for you." At that moment, she ran into the restroom to compose herself. When she came back out, she told me that she couldn't do "this" anymore and that she was leaving the industry.

All it took was one person reminding her of her true identity and God's unfailing love for her to make the decision to remove herself from a destructive lifestyle. I know, without a doubt, that God used us as an answer to her family's prayers.

LABEL REMOVAL

The devil wants the girls at the convention to believe that "once a porn star, always a porn star." He wants the porn addicted to believe they can never be whole, the pimp and producer to think they can never be forgiven, and the director and the camera man to think their creativity will never be used for something clean and filled with purpose. The labels the enemy tattoos on the hearts and minds of the captives in this industry are very real to them, but not to the God who made them.

When we speak to people in the porn industry, we give them truth that will bring them the knowledge of God. The church word for it is *prophecy,* since prophecy is speaking God's word of identity and purpose by strengthening, encouraging, and comforting the hearer. Of course, we can't use the term prophecy with people who disregard anything churchy, so God gave us the term "Label Removal."

Tapping into the Spirit of Truth, we get words of knowledge (also called "downloads") about derogatory terms they have labeled themselves with, or labels that have been put on them by others. Regardless of age, people tend to identify with their label instead of the truth of their identity. That tendency is on hyperdrive in the porn industry.

So, how does label removal work? Two ways: either they tell you the labels they feel describe their identity or you tell them the negative labels you see and would like to remove from them.

An example label would be something like "you are a failure." The deeper connotations are "you are a bad person," "you never learn," "you will never amount to anything," "you are a liar," and just about any negative thing that would come to mind. That's when you flip it around and tell them, "you're loved," "you're valuable," "you have an important purpose," and other words of truth that God leads you to say Whatever Satan means for evil, God uses for good. What does God say about them? It's always the opposite of what they believe. Where they see condemnation, He sees holiness. Tell them what He sees.

Whatever label they give or label you see on them, proclaim the opposite. Because words have power, you can prophesy a destiny over them and completely destroy the works of Satan over their lives. You can remove horrible labels from their hearts and minds and turn them around, cutting away words spoken out of anger or brokenness. I'm not kidding when I say the Holy Spirit gives all of us the ability to craft words of affirmation, edification, and comfort. It seems we always speak just the right affirming and uplifting words they need to hear. As Job 22:28 says:

> You will also declare a thing,
> And it will be established for you;
> So light will shine on your ways.

Proverbs 18:21 says, "Death and life are in the power of the tongue." So, use words to break off negative, horrible, destructive things and cancel Satan's assignment over them. They can then connect to the Spirit of Truth and experience the life God designed them to have.

KEY THINGS TO REMEMBER

As you converse with seekers and lead them through these tools, *actively* listen to the Holy Spirit. Our role is to introduce people to the Spirit of Truth, not be the Guru ourselves. God works through us so that people get to the point where they are open to accepting what God has for them. Respect the process. God works in people's lives in unique ways. Our job is to water the soil, and sometimes we won't be the one seeing the fruit in someone's life. God likely has many other people he wants to use in that person's life.

You may be the third, seventh, or thirtieth person that God

GOD'S HEART FOR THE SEEKERS

uses to draw someone to Him, so don't jump the gun. Value what the other person values. When someone shares their values and experiences with you, say something like, "That's interesting. Tell me more about that!" This searching element on your end lowers a bridge for conversation and community. Remember that their culture is completely different than yours. Asking them about something they value helps you learn about their culture and reflects the love of the Father.

God was the one who taught me these words that work. I did evangelism incorrectly for so many years until I listened to the techniques and language that God wanted to use to reach His children. Be wise and watch the language you use. By doing this, we bypass the walls of hurt and affect people on a spiritual level. Remember that the truth of God's love and Personhood is not confined to Christianese terminology. God has many ways to express Himself, especially in light of the new and foreign culture we live in today.

Although our team often uses dream interpretation and prophecy to interact with seekers, you don't need to be a dream interpreter to connect people to God. By sharing their true identity with them and listening to what the Holy Spirit is telling you about that person, you can be a source of radical, godly love in their journey toward the heavenly Father. If you want to learn how to interpret dreams, I encourage you to read my book *What Your Dreams Are Telling You* and see how the Lord wants to use you in that area. No matter what, when you are actively listening to the Holy Spirit as a strategic cultural ambassador, God will use you to bring Him glory.

A NOTE ON TEAM UNITY AND PRAYER

I must address the team element of outreach because it's so important. Every team member of our outreach groups agrees to model unity and love toward one another. We have a "no disunity" policy in our team building. We work as one and maintain peace, love, and respect for one another.

Each team member assembles their own intercessors who agree to pray for them before, during, and after the outreach event. We select one main leader of the prayer teams so the group of people praying for that one team member also prays for the whole team. The lead prayer member has all the contact information of the prayer teams. We communicate with the lead prayer person during the event, who then sends out prayer requests to all the groups of prayer participants.

The people who intercede for us while we are on the outreach can often number upwards of three hundred. This divine communication is so important. We would not be able to do our outreaches without continual covering and team unity. Whenever you are on outreach, make sure that you are continually covered in prayer and intercession.

TEAM BUILDING AND INTERCESSORS

The teams I lead are one in heart, purpose, function, spirit, unity, and love for each other and our guests. We have a no-tolerace policy for rebellion, disunity, or disrespect. We honor and prefer others first. Our teams model unity, forgiveness, and kindness. We are not rude to each other, and we do not get into heated arguments about anything.

We come to an event with an open mind to learn more about God's love and we have never reached its depth. Our understanding is realized when we see that where sin abounds, grace really does much more abound.

We have an "Intercessor General" each year who has all the names of the intercessors for each team member, and that general receives communication from me and our leaders about the needs or updates as we have them and then sends it out to all the intercessors. That way, everyone at home knows how it's going and what to pray for. We are flexible and honoring to each other. We seek to model His character and love at all times.

OTHER TOOLS OF OUTREACH

Other than dreams, one of the tools we use at places we go are rubber wristbands with affirmative words on them such as "You have purpose," "You have identity," and "You are loved." We tell event goers to pick a color and almost everyone gladly accepts. As they put them on, we tell them their "future forecast." We call it a "no-brainer" word of knowledge. Once they pick a color, we read the words of affirmation out loud and place it on their wrist. We tell them:

"This is your future forecast. You have a purpose, and this is it…"

"This is for you. You have a gift of…"

"You have worth, and this is what I know about you…"

The Lord would allow us to see into their hearts and tell them His original purpose. We always give them something to hold onto so that the silly little rubber bracelet would remind them of the positive word we spoke into them. For the first time in a long time, they hear the truth about themselves and it feels good—so good that it sticks with them.

The first time we did this at the porn convention, before the outreach I had gotten a download of a roulette wheel with colored sections. We created positive words to write on each color and created wristbands to match the color. The color and message they landed on was their future forecast. We read the words on the wristband out loud as we put it on their wrist. More often than not, the words they landed on were words they had just used in their conversations before they spun the wheel.

Before too long, we were quadruple booked with people standing in front of our booth to spin the wheel. The booths around us were selling merchandise that one would expect at a porn convention, but we had the most popular booth at the event. The language on the wristbands were:

Red: YOU HAVE VALUE, PURPOSE & YOU ARE LOVED
Hot pink: HAPPINESS AND HARMONY
Green: DREAMS—EMPOWER
Light blue: FAITH—ENVISION
Orange: DETERMINATION—COURAGE
Purple: FREEDOM—SPIRIT
Yellow: STRENGTH—SUCCESS
Navy blue: GOALS—FULFILLMENT

GOD'S HEART FOR THE SEEKERS

By the time we were wrapping up the event, there were so many people wearing the wristbands. Probably over half of the 25,000 people who attended had one. Our booth had become so popular that a CEO from another adult convention asked us to come to his and gave us a booth for half of the cost. When God gives you an idea, He also gives you favor that opens up other doors. Each idea God gives us comes with a "compelling" element to give people an opportunity to hear a word of hope and encouragement from God. They are starving for it.

Recently, we had one person on our team encounter a young porn star who said, "Oh, my gosh. I remember you from last year." She told everyone else to go away, including people wanting to take her picture and bring her water, because she needed twenty minutes with our team. When she was finally alone, she told us, "You told me things last year that have absolutely transformed my life. I am getting ready to get out and make a change in my life."

This transformation started with a rubber bracelet that opened a door for a word of identity that sparked something in her heart.

The final thing I'll say about going behind enemy lines at porn conventions is this: because these people are so immersed in a culture of hyper sexualization, their true self craves something clean, real, and innocent. They can put on their makeup and do their hair; they can don a suit and seductive sunglasses, but we see through that façade. Nobody ever grew up wanting this lifestyle of perversion.

That's why they crave hugs from me and my team We love them through the clean love of the Holy Spirit. It's pure and carries no expectations. People feel that deep down and sometimes literally follow us throughout the venue, looking for an opportunity to let us embrace them again and again.

I think we are answers to silent or long-forgotten prayers as we go into some of these arenas. The thing I have found, especially in the porn conventions, is that a lot of the young girls are looking for a mom. They are looking for someone to be available to them who will love them and not want something dirty or sexual from them. Several years ago, three girls chased us out of the door at the very end of the convention and asked if they could get one more hug. "Of course you can!" we said.

Do not judge. Love. Love and watch them, because when you hug someone, it is the arms of Jesus hugging them. You can see and feel the shift in the atmosphere and their demeanor as the clean love of Jesus flows through you to them.

I believe the mother in me is what they connect with. A true mom hug unlocks so much hurt, allows walls to melt, and brings acceptance. There's actually an art to it. We make sure we stand literally heart to heart and give them a full, steady embrace. We don't let go until they do, which is sometimes several minutes.

Can you imagine how relieved they are that someone is actually giving to them instead of taking from them? It's powerful. Sometimes I come undone along with them as I speak life into them. Lots of tears are shed, but they are good, cleansing tears that wash some of the pain away.

CHAPTER 11

IT'S FUN TO BUILD BRIDGES

I have come to enjoy New Age bookstores. Since New Agers are already in tune with spiritual things, they are easy to introduce to the Spirit of Truth. On any given day, you can go to a New Age bookstore and find tarot card readers, mediums, palm readers, and even witches giving readings, interpreting dreams, and consulting spirits. They're right out in the open. Anyone can listen in, so I do. That's when the Holy Spirit really goes to work.

Whether it's a spiritual reading or dream interpretation, I can always hear the bondage these practitioners are laying on the seekers at their tables. Warnings of premature death, dark and confusing instructions, and just plain disinformation lead these mystics and creatives in circles. They are going nowhere fast, and it grieves the Holy Spirit so much that He downloads amazing, detailed information to me while I'm eavesdropping.

As a heavenly hitman, I will hang out nearby, praying in tongues while pretending to be interested in a book on incantations or meditation. Once the seeker has left the table, I walk up and say, "I heard what they told you, but you need to know that the Spirit of Truth revealed to me something amazing about your purpose and destiny. Do you want to know what He said?" The answer is always yes. They are starving for truth! They are desperate for a life-giving word that touches their heart instead of giving them a heart attack.

I'll stay in a bookstore for a few hours at a time and pick off everyone I can. It's so much fun to introduce these creatives and philosophers to the One who created them. Many times, they literally get hit by the Spirit. Some have fallen out under the power of the Holy Ghost right there in the bookstore. Through the encounter, they know they've met Truth and that truth is Jesus.

Many times, I act as a disruptor. While I've prayed in tongues nearby, I've heard many psychics say, "I don't know what's wrong with me today. The spirits are usually so clear, but I'm just not hearing from them. I just feel a real interference, so I'm going to call it a day and try again tomorrow."

Once they leave, there is an open chair for me to interpret dreams, prophesy over people, and give them words of knowledge from the true source. In each instance, the person gets a true encounter with the One who created them. This is just one of the many tools my teams and I use to reach these spiritual sojourners, many of whom are witches and warlocks.

Just like porn conventions, we need to go into New Age stores and metaphysics fairs focused on the hearts of the people the Holy Spirit has lined up for us to meet. We don't know how these people came to be witches, psychics, or spiritual sojourners, but there is always a divine purpose for the way they are meant to live. That's what my team and I are looking for. These are the questions we ask ourselves:

- How does Jesus want to reach this person?
- How does He want to bring them into who they are really meant to be?
- What gifts did He put in them that we can connect to or draw out?

When I first started going into these dark places, God told me that if I put my finger on the pulse of culture, He would bring me encounters with people who need Him. Because I know my steps are ordered by Him, I understand that every time I go out, it's a Holy Spirit setup. He's gone before us and warmed up the crowd.

Because Jesus is a friend to sinners, we purpose in our hearts and minds to go as friends—no judgment or condemnation. We just get to say, "Tell me about your life. Tell me about yourself so we can get to know you." The results of these conversations, often at our booth or table, lead us in many fun and interesting directions.

For example, we once met a masseuse who was into New Age practices. She had consulted crystals, Ouija boards, and whatever else, so I went and got a massage from her. I remember people saying, "You can't go in there and get a massage from her because if she touches you, you're going to be infected."

"Wait a minute," I said. "The greater One lives on the inside of me, so if she's touching me, I'm touching her, and the God inside me is actually touching her." So I went to get the massage anyway. While some great instrumental music played in the background, I noticed that she suddenly wasn't touching me anymore. I looked back and saw that she was doing circles with her fingers extended in the air above my back.

"What are you doing?" I asked.

"Energy work," she said. "Can you feel it?"

"No, I can't," I told her, and noticed that she had three places on both arms that looked like symmetrical bruises. She had one on her wrists, one on the middle of her arms, and one on her shoulders.

I said, "What on earth did you do? Did you fall down?"

"No," she said, "I don't know what this is. It just started happening."

I could tell she was a seeker that gave her entire heart to crystals and meditation. She'd put her whole heart into helping absorb customers' energy. It seemed like the bruises were some kind of physical manifestation of that.

"I don't understand what happened," she said, "I meditated

on a crystal and asked the triangle, and the triangle spelled out a mustard herb. I went down to Whole Foods store and got the mustard herb, crushed it up, and put it on my skin, but it burned me."

"You know, oftentimes the Creator uses me as an energy healer," I said, using her words back on her. "Would you like for me to do that on you?"

"Oh, yes, I would love that! Thank you," she replied, so I asked God, "Where do you want me to put my hand?"

"Put it on her spot on her shoulder," He said. I put my hand on her shoulder and of course it got hot. She said, "I feel that.

"I know, right?" I replied. Oftentimes when the energy from the Creator is working, it literally creates a heat component that goes along with it.

"Another thing's coming to me," I continued. "People are beginning to do a thing called a Psalm reading. What you do is you take the oldest book in the in the world and right at the center on the inside is a book called Psalms. It's poetic, it's melodic, and it's got a lot of real positive information in there. I'm told that if you read these words out loud in that book of Psalms, it literally goes back over you and heals all of your flesh."

"That's amazing," she replied.

"You know, people are getting groups together and they're starting to do this. They're reading it out loud as a group almost like a meditation process."

"That's amazing," she repeated.

"I know," I said, smiling, "it's becoming very popular."

"I'm going to do it."

I said, "I think you should. It's a Bible, so you're gonna open it straight up into the middle to the book of Psalms and it has these really positive, energy-healing words that come out of it."

I went back to her another time and she said, "I have to tell you how much this has meant. This is transforming my life, making me awake and aware now."

We must remember that there are people that are saved and those that are being saved. Sometimes we just have to build the bridge. Sometimes we just have to love them enough for the bridge to go down. They need to know that we're a safe place and we're not going to be beating them up because they live a life different and apart from God.

It's important to be open to the many different ways that God connects with seekers. If you listen to the way people are wired and you hear the Holy Spirit, God will tell you what to say to them no matter what.

I was in a little mining town in California one time, and we decided that we'd do some dreams. It was a really spiritually active little town, so there were all kinds of New Age shops. I walked into one of them and met an artist. She had all this beautiful glass artwork displayed in her shop and she had on all kinds of colors. Over her head I saw purple and blue. God gave me an insight into what she likes.

I told her what I saw, and it immediately got her attention. "I love purple and blue," she said enthusiastically. "I'm the goddess of summer." She kept going with a nonsense answer. As I was looking at her, the Lord spoke to me in that moment and said, "She speaks fairy tale."

I thought, *Oh, okay,* then looked at her and said, "While you're saying this, I'm reminded of a story of a King that had a son. The son was so in love with the Kingdom that he died. He decided he would pierce himself and he would allow the blood in the healing ointment flow out of his hand. The son died for the Kingdom because he loved it so much."

I felt my hand get hot, so I reached out and put it on her heart. The healing went through her and she began weeping. "I know," I said as she felt the healing power of God on her. She'd understood the message of Jesus because God directed me to put the redemption story into language that made sense to her.

I encourage you to just go with it when God gives you insight on how to share Himself with someone. I'm sure He enjoys seeing us walk out in this. He might even be sitting there telling the angels, "Get over here. You've got to come watch!"

BEAUTIFUL PEOPLE, BROKEN PEOPLE

Although you would never guess it, the folks at Sundance who seem to have the world at their feet are some of the most insecure people on the planet. Everything around them is fake: Fake names, fake relationships, fake noses, fake chins, you name it. Life in a fantasy world is anything but fantastic because there is never anything real. They never have anything solid to grasp or true to hang your hat on. The men and women inhabiting Sundance are not just there to hustle their movies and garner attention. They are on a quest for something authentic. We give that to them.

When people ask me, "Are all dreams from God?" My answer is always, "No, but God made every dreamer." We can expect He will use our dreams to send us personal messages, instructions, warnings, and light for our path. When we interpret dreams, we awaken the dreamer to the fact that the One who made them can and will communicate to them when they are sleeping.

One of my favorite stories from Sundance, which I told in my book *What Your Dreams Are Telling You*, was a young man from Hollywood who came into our nook in a coffee shop with an entourage of friends. He definitely stood out as the alpha male of the pack. Everyone followed him. His personal style and sense of bravado were obviously his hallmark traits. Was he an actor or the child of a famous person? We still don't know.

When the pack came in, I caught his eye and he said, "I had a dream." His friends said, "You did! Tell her about it."

The next thing I knew, the group was at my table. The young man said, "I had a dream that I was driving my car, wrecked it, and died. I was instantly standing before the judgment seat of Christ. I looked at Him, then I saw two lines. One line was going to heaven, one was going to hell, and I was in the middle."

By this time, all of his friends were glued to hearing what this dream could mean. He then asked me, "Am I going to die?" I stared at him for a minute and answered, "Yes!" His friends were in shock. They said, "Dude, you're gonna die?"

I looked at each of them and said, "Yes! We're all going to die. The good news about your dream is that you get to decide which line you are going to be in before you die." At that point, he sat back smugly in the chair and said, "Well, I don't really believe in God."

"Well, dude, it was *your* dream." He had no escape then. I said, "I didn't have it. The message is for you, not me."

I realized how amazingly sneaky God is. In this young man telling his dream, he accurately communicated to all of his friends the existence of God, a final judgment day, and only two choices you can make in determining which line you will be in when you die. I was loving it! Talk about a God setup.

As he and his friends got up to leave, God assured me that this was not the only dream he would have. It wasn't the time to tell him about Jesus. He was in shock at the moment. Besides, Jesus was doing a pretty good job of telling him about Himself through his dreams.

"Let me be absolutely clear," I told him. "God speaks to us all through dreams, and I'm sure God gave you this dream for a reason. Know that He doesn't give you dreams like this to scare you, but to prepare you. He's giving you an opportunity right now to say yes."

In short, that young man walked away seriously thinking about his eternal fate. Many of his buddies stayed and got themselves saved. I count it as a great big win for Jesus because I know the Holy Spirit was working on him and continued long after he walked out that door.

STAND AND DELIVER

When we interpret a dream on the streets or give some sort of spiritual encounter, we will often do a thing we call "Standing Deliverance." It is a very simple thing I learned early on as God was teaching me new ways to reach the ones He loves. I simply ask a person if they would give me permission to ask the Creator to remove everything from them that would keep them from fulfilling their destiny. I have never had anyone tell me no.

This gives me the opportunity to use my creative language God gave me to bind things and to loose things on this earth, just like what Jesus says in Matthew 16:19. I also access the authority Jesus gave me to cancel every dark demonic work or pathway of destruction that has been made against them. When they agree with me to give the Creator permission to remove everything from them that would keep them from fulfilling their destiny, they have just given God permission to define His life for them.

The god of this world, Satan, no longer has permission to lie, to steal, or to destroy them. We must begin to believe God's word and use the gifts and authority He says we have. If Jesus gave us authority over all the works of darkness, then we have full authority in Him to completely cancel every assignment of hell over the people that He is so desperate to reach.

Hollywood is often called "The Dream Factory," but I

know the true source of dreams and messages in night seasons: the One who created us. Dreams are a very effective tool He uses to communicate with us directly.

I have run into so many people, especially at the Sundance Film Festival, who did not recognize their dream was coming from a divine source, so they were actually scared by it. Some of them did not want to go to sleep for fear of having a dream they didn't understand or one that might actually come true. Dreaming about things that come true scares a lot of people. They don't have a clue how to handle it and feel creeped out. What they don't realize is that they have a gift that is activated by a divine source. It gives them more than information. It gives them a foresight—a kind of window into the future. Jesus will do that even if someone doesn't know Him personally yet.

We know time does not exist in heaven. Heaven is in eternity. God created time for us, and Isaiah 46:10 says He knows "the end from the beginning." That means He can see it all at once and He already knows our last breath. Consequently, sometimes people can see things way ahead of time when they connect with the Giver of the dream. This makes it even more powerful. Prophetic gifts are something people can be born with, but they are also something that works better when they connect with the One who put them together.

REALITY CHECK

I hear people talk about "pizza dreams." These are dreams people believe have no real meaning because they were caused by indigestion or some other strange source. In this day and age, we often give television, movies, social media, or video games credit for the content of our dreams. I hear people say, "I must have dreamed that because I saw a movie last week that reminded me of it." Little do they know that the God of the universe is trying to reach them.

When it comes to young people spending all their time plugged into some device, it is really disturbing because they are being conditioned. Their minds are being taught that fantasy is reality. Many can't distinguish between acceptable social behavior and the kind of behavior they see in video games or TV shows. A chasm is forming as children are being raised on a steady diet of sensory violence, disrespect, and self-gratification. This is a time when we need to have the best of intentions toward one another, not violence, hatred, or disregard.

Dreams seem to come from two different sources—a God source or an evil source. When we overload on negativity, violence, sexual content, and extreme fantasy, we're inviting demonic dreams of confusion, darkness, and despair. Because we are sleeping and therefore vulnerable while in a dream state, seeds of deception can be planted in our minds that stay with us when we wake up.

Each one of us has a responsibility to guard our own heart, choose life over death and blessings over curses. I think we need to be very careful about what kind of mental and spiritual seeds we are sowing into ourselves and our children. We need to make sure we are not watering—paying attention to and nurturing—things that are going to grow into weeds, stickers, and thorns in our lives.

GOD ALWAYS DELIVERS

Looking for a new avenue in which to reach God's friends at Sundance, I wandered into a New Age store. After speaking briefly with them, I was surprised and a little apprehensive when they told me they wanted us to "practice dream interpretation on some of their friends." What they were really saying was, "Just how good are you?"

I was immediately intimidated. I thought, *Oh, no! We are new to this. We are practicing, not proficient.* But I knew I couldn't back out now, so I went back to my little team. We prayed and asked the Lord to not only give us interpretation of their dreams, but tell us what the dream was even before they could tell us. That is what God did for Daniel with King Nebuchadnezzar's dream in Daniel 2. Amazingly, He did! He gave us the interpretation of the dream and the contents of the dream before they told us about it.

The owner of the shop, a hardcore New Ager, was scratching his head. "Cindy," he said, visibly perplexed, "I have never seen anything like this before. I've never even heard of anything like this before. You and your team are the most gifted dream interpreters I've ever seen."

He even asked how many dreams we needed to interpret correctly be able to qualify for a master certification. Suddenly confident, I informed him, "One thousand." He opened his store for our dream team to interpret dreams two Thursday nights each month for two years. We lived in Utah, so it was a good gig for us. He was so impressed that he would send out announcements promoting us to his mailing list of 18,000 people.

The people came and endured some pretty long wait times. That's how important it was for them to get a clear interpretation of their dreams. We were able to communicate the reality of Jesus in a whole new arena. People were searching for the Way, the Truth, and the Life and just didn't know He was what they wanted.

To this day, if I put up a sign saying "Dream Interpretation Here," people will line up and patiently wait their turn. That's how much they want answers.

We must operate according to the season and the time we are placed in. We have to. Since 1973, I have watched myself fail miserably many times because I didn't recognize the new thing God was doing. I have watched myself do things out of my own zeal— again, we cannot let our zeal get ahead of the love of God.

The love of God is peaceful. It is pure. It is like wisdom and is easily understood. The love of God is a wonderful, rushing river that brings people to the place of repentance through its kindness. It brings them to the point where they realize they have a safe place to share their thoughts and be themselves. It's like this:

> I have a safe place to tell you what I have been doing. I need for you to help me. I trust you and I want you to

explain to me. Give me the words of life. Give me a new direction. Give me something I can live for and hope for.

SELFLESS LOVE THAT TRANSFORMS

Mira was a single Christian mom who had only one adult son named David. David was living in a same-sex relationship with his partner, Marcus. Mira was an older, praying woman and David was the only family she had left. Even though Mira had hoped for David to marry and give her grandchildren, David had chosen this alternate lifestyle, which went against his mother's beliefs.

Mira had a choice to make regarding her son and his partner. She could have been angry and distanced herself from her son, but because of her love for David, she chose to love him right where he was at, even having family dinners with David and Marcus. Not too long in her son's relationship with his partner, Marcus became ill. David asked his mother to come with him to the doctor, and they learned Marcus had developed the AIDS virus. David was devastated and Mira went straight to God in prayer seeking direction and counsel to know what to do with this diagnosis and how to pray for Marcus.

God asked Mira to take Marcus and David into her home. Mira became Marcus's caregiver, and David worked to support the family. Mira cooked for them, gave Marcus his medication, cleaned his wounds, and kept company with Marcus as his health declined. Each time she cared for Marcus using his medications on his wounds, she would silently pray for him. Peace would settle over him, causing Marcus to feel God's presence and unconditional love for him.

Marcus had come from a very broken home, even living with foster families for portions of his life. In Marcus's early years, he experienced a very turbulent upbringing filled with abuse—sexual, physical, and mental. He was filled with memories of abandonment, rejection, and confusion. Each day Mira spent time with Marcus, she learned more and more about his tragic past and with each story, Mira developed more and more compassion for Marcus.

The day came when Marcus's disease had advanced, and Mira and David knew that without a miracle, he would die. Mira had become a very close friend to Marcus and a trust had formed between them. Two days before he died, Marcus asked Mira if Jesus loved him like she did and if he would be able to go to heaven. Mira assured him that Jesus absolutely loved him no matter what, and at that moment, Marcus asked Jesus into his heart. David was on one side of the bed and Mira was on the other side of the bed when Marcus said a simple heart-felt prayer and told them that he felt as if his life had just begun. All three wept, prayed, and sang as they experienced God's loving presence in the room.

This is the love that never fails. David asked Jesus to restore his life, make him new, and for God to forgive him for turning his back to Him. The day Marcus died, Mira and David were changed forever. They had experienced God's unfailing love. They had a new understanding of a Savior who looks on people's hearts and loves people without judgment and condemnation. They both had a greater concept of God who is a loving Father and will go to any length to heal, restore, and rescue anyone from anyplace by any method He can.

At the end of his life, a lesson was learned. To put it plainly, we don't know people's stories. We don't know what they have been through, nor what their pain was like to cause them to choose one path or another. People are looking for acceptance, unconditional love, and a safe place to ask for help from a life of trauma to find a God whose love has no limits. Jesus will go to any length to rescue them and longs to breathe life into them.

MASSIVE LIGHT OUTREACH

We were in downtown Dallas recently with a new outreach we created called Massive Light. We interpreted dreams and gave the lines of people eager for a spiritual encounter through True Reflections. People were so hungry that they were asking us to give them hope and something to hold onto.

We look at most dreams with a redeemed interpretation because God does not speak death into us. We told the seekers, "Look, God has got you. You just need to let Him in and let Him give you peace. Let Him give you life. You need to surrender to Jesus and know He is going to direct and guide your path. He is going to straighten things out, just as he says in Isaiah 45:2: 'I will go before you and make the crooked places straight.'"

We could have stayed there for hours. Why? Because

people tell us they do not know what to do now. They have no idea the time or the season. They have no wisdom, understanding, or insight. They're stuck and they know it.

When the Holy Spirit fills us with power (and I have certainly felt it come on me recently), my prophetic gift operates like crazy. I hear Holy Spirit downloads of words that were said in a home before the person ever came to see me on the street. That is a Daniel thing, and it is extreme.

I'm ready for this. I want to see this happen, but I also want to be wise. I want to be like the sons of Issachar where I understand the times and the seasons, and I know what I am supposed to do. I know what we are coming up against and I know how quickly things are moving. I know what God is asking us to do, but I do not want to jump the gun.

THERE IS NO CONDEMNATION

People need to repent. People need to get their lives straightened out, but shaming them does not and will never work. When there is a season of Holy Spirit outpouring on the earth, *conviction* comes with it, not condemnation.

There is a difference between conviction and condemnation. Conviction will bring a person to their knees, just like the great revivals with those revivalists like Maria Woodsworth-Etter, Kathryn Kuhlmann, William Branum, Charles Finney, and Evan Roberts. Those revivals were a season of outpouring that people flocked to because they needed to get their lives right.

The preachers and evangelists did not have to scream at them and tell them to repent. The seekers knew to repent and were ready because the conviction of the Holy Spirit was on them to do so. When our Christlike love is obvious and the message is right, it is even more critical to be in sync with the season and the time.

CHAPTER 12

THEY WILL KNOW US BY OUR LOVE

The Jesus Movement was wonderful. We had brand-new lives and operated in gifts. We saw healings and witnessed every kind of miracle. Along with it all, there was a presence that hovered over us. The atmosphere was electric with His love and power. You literally felt the Holy Spirit.

I believe that is what is coming. It is going to be similar to it, except it is going to be more like a lion. It is going to come with some very serious ultimatums.

Why? Because we are living in times when deep darkness covers the earth. There is a deep darkness enveloping people, and we are to arise and shine. God's light is going to shine on us and He's going to equip us with power. He is going to cover us and ignite us with power. When we go out, we are going to see unusual occurrences, signs, wonders, and miracles. We are going to be able to watch God embrace the ones He loves.

But beware. If we don't do this with love, we are no better than giant noisemaker. First Corinthians 13:1–3 says:

> Though I speak with the tongues of men and of angels, but have not love, I have become sounding brass or a clanging cymbal. And though I have the gift of prophecy, and understand all mysteries and all knowledge, and though I have all faith, so that I could remove mountains, but have not love, I am nothing. And though I bestow all my goods to feed the poor, and though I give my body to be burned, but have not love, it profits me nothing.

Nobody is going to be saved if it is not done with love. It's like the old saying, "Nobody cares what you know until they know you care." It's like that with the Kingdom. It's the love of God that brings men to change—the place where folks feel safe enough to confess and connect to God.

NEW WINESKINS FOR NEW WINE

How do we prepare for the new wineskin, this new Great Awakening era? Spend time with the Lord. Understand His Word. Use this time to get with God and experience the Holy Spirit. Learn how He talks to us. We are going to need it. We are going to need to know what the Bible says. If you don't know where things are in the Bible, you need to look them up.

I'm not trying to scare you. I'm trying to prepare you.

I am aware of a coming closeness with the Lord like never before. I am just getting the lay of the land. I feel the prophetic really creeping up on the inside of me. I am having experiences in the prophetic realm like I have not had in years. I know something is getting ready to happen. I encourage you to be ready for when things do happen.

I want to remind you to not let your zeal get in the way or get ahead of the love of God. You will completely ruin your outreach if you do that. Your zeal gets you nowhere. The love of God is patient, kind, and easy to be understood. It follows you. It goes with you. It is calm. It is a still, small voice that gives you understanding. You receive divine wisdom, knowledge, and divine revelation. You begin to understand. You know where things are, what things are happening, and you are not taken off base by fear or any kind of knee-jerk reaction that could cause offense.

We *must* do evangelism God's way. When we do, we see tremendous results. We are coming up on the new season. It is like a tsunami we know is coming. We watch for it. We listen for it. We're alert and sensitive to it, then we see it on the horizon. It is coming! When it does, it comes with power!

Will you be swept up in this tsunami and carried to your purpose in life and destiny for Jesus, or will you be crushed by it, unable to move forward because you were not prepared (or refused) to jump on the wave? If you don't get with God's program for this last generation, you will be crushed under the weight of not fulfilling your purpose.

Like I said earlier, you have free will. You can choose to live out every step of your purpose and destiny, or you can find a comfortable couch and watch someone else bring in the harvest that was meant for you. It's your choice, but it is not without consequence to you or to the world around you. Right now is your Esther 4:14 moment:

> "For if you remain completely silent at this time, relief and deliverance will arise for the Jews from another place, but you and your father's house will perish. Yet who knows whether you have come to the kingdom for such a time as this?"

We live in a world that is starving for spiritual truth, identity, and direction. People aimlessly wander around trying to figure out life. Without a vision, people die. Thankfully, there is an answer in Jesus. It's time to get real, deal with stuff, and step into our identity as the sons and daughters of a loving, forgiving Father who is willing to help us become whole. Good character is a must. It only comes from seeking His face in prayer and developing a healthy fear of the Lord, which is our anchor for growing in all aspects.

God has been teaching me His way of reaching people who would never come to church. During my time at Burning Man, New Age fairs, film festivals, pagan events, and adult conventions, God taught me things about the world we actually live in and His heart for the people He made. He taught me about myself and challenged me to leave my old way of thinking about outreach and embrace new ideas, new methods, and new understanding of how He is moving in the current culture. We all have the pull to lean on our own understanding when it comes to teaching and learning about God. In all of my experiences, however, God has shown me that His ways and thoughts are vastly different than mine.

A NEW NORMAL

It all starts with relationships, which has not been the normal protocol for past revivals. You and I need to befriend seekers of truth regardless of where they come from or what they stand for. We are in a time of building bridges with people who think differently than we do. We need to value them and hear their stories. We do not know what they have been through. If hurtful or harsh words of condemnation are spoken to them, even out of a place of love, it could repel them away.

I just love that Holy Spirit teaches us how to follow Jesus. He teaches us how to do what the Father wants done. We need to align ourselves with God and ask Him, "What are we going to do? I'm going to say what you say. I'm going to think what you think. I'm going to go where you go. I'm going to align myself with you because you know that person. You know those areas. You know the places where these people have been. I'm aligning myself with you and asking you to impart information and give me compassion by the way of the Holy Spirit. Give me love to speak to that person so there is a radical change in their thinking and life."

I have seen it happen over and over again—love is the motivating factor in people connecting with the Spirit of Truth. Love is so powerful! A great compassion wells up in me that I know is not my own. I do not have that kind of compassion naturally. We do not have a radical kind of love, but Jesus does, and He has no problem sharing it with us.

When that love joins with perfect timing and Holy Spirit power, you can point to someone from ten feet away and they will fall over under the power of God. You can explain redemption in language they understand. You can go into the darkest places and bring the greatest Light.

APPENDIX

SAY THIS AND NOT THAT

Here are some alternate words and phrases you can use to help you communicate with the world outside of church. Note that some of the more negative-sounding Christian terminology has been flipped to the positive. We do this because we want to build up seekers and encourage them in their walk, going against the burdens of the enemy that have pulled them down for so long. Note that the meanings of these two columns are exactly the same. We're not changing or removing the incredible truth of Jesus, only explaining it with different words. It's incredible that a small vocabulary change can have such a profound effect on seekers' openness to the gospel.

Christian Language	Words That Work
Advocate	Defender; the One who fights our battles when we can't
Ancient of Days	Ancient One; foundational wise counselor
Anointing	You have a special ability.
Assignment	You have a job to do.
Authority	You have the ability to influence others.
Baptism in the Holy Spirit	New power and spirit language
Bible	Blueprint for life, written to guide us; Spirit-inspired guidebook for all things pertaining to life and right living; Keeps us from falling into destructive pits designed to destroy us; Life words that tell us about God and Jesus and the world He made for us and the afterlife
Blessing	Good things are coming out of you and on you.
Blood of Jesus	Red purifying life flow
Bondage	Feeling trapped or hindered
Born again or born-again experience	Spiritual awakening; organic restart; organic new start for life
Burdens, heavy weights	Innocence restorer; deeper inner healing and canceling soul ties

SAY THIS AND NOT THAT

Christian Language	Words That Work
Call of God	Destiny, purpose, and reason you are here
Calling	Uniquely gifted and set apart for a special purpose
Canceling Satan's assignments	Peace imparting; casting out fear
Casting our care on Him; His yoke is easy and His burden is light	The Trauma Remover provides inner healing in the mind and emotions.
Check in your spirit	Something seems off; feeling a warning
Cleansing	Refining, healing, and leaving behind old habits
Condemnation and guilt	The Shame Taker speaks truth over them, ridding them of bearing shame for past mistakes and wrongdoing.
Confusion	Clouded thoughts producing anxiety
Dead in their sins	The Life Infuser breathes life into dead areas of their being, especially emotionally.
Declarations	Life words; power of life by speaking Truth
Deliverance	Spiritual cleansing
Demons	A negative force working against you

WORDS THAT WORK

Christian Language	Words That Work
Disciple	A student learning spiritual things of truth
Edification	Encouragement
Enemy	A dark force
Even before you were formed in the womb, I knew you, every hair on your head is numbered	Identity definer; the One who made you defines your identity
Faith	Trust in something you can't see but you know will happen
Favor	Good things coming your way
Fear	Emotional prison created from past negative experiences
Fearfully and wonderfully made	Original root recovery; removal of false identities and false directions to discover our original self
Forgiveness	Forgiver, where bad things are removed from a person and no longer remembered
Fruit	Evidence of good outcomes from things you have done
God speaks one way, then another, in a dream or vision in the night	Giver of dreams; God's instructions and guidance while we sleep
Grace	Things are going to be easier.

SAY THIS AND NOT THAT

Christian Language	Words That Work
Have you ever stolen, lied, or cheated?	All of us have lived lives that have separated us from absolute Love, who is God. We aren't identified by the wrong things we have done, because the One who made us looks on our hearts and is relentless to bring us into safety and His arms again.
Heaven	Yes, the word *heaven* is usable in most cases! However, you can describe it as an eternal place where there is no sorrow, pain, or suffering, just unexplainable joy, life, peace, love; it really does exist.
He is near to the broken hearted	Heart transformations; hearts made whole and completely restored
Hell	A place where evil's torment is nonstop. It's a real place after death, where there is no escape. It really does exist, but if your life is surrendered to Jesus and He lives in you and you in Him, you will not see it.
He makes all things new	True reflections done with a mirror to see who someone truly is and proclaim the original good roots

WORDS THAT WORK

Christian Language	Words That Work
He makes crooked places straight and rough places smooth	The Path Illuminator makes solid, untwisted pathways and straight, unhindered paths
Holiness	A purifying Spiritual alignment
Holy Spirit	Spirit of Truth
Hopeless	Life restorer; God's presence restores life
I am a Christian	Jesus guides my life, mind, and pathway. His supernatural pure nature lives inside of me.
Infilling of the Holy Spirit after deliverance	Redefinement
Inner healing	Trauma removal
Jesus	The Way, path direction; Life replacing death; Truth, revealing lies; Light, illuminating darkness; Shame Taker; Peace; Mercy; Healer; Ancient One; Wisdom; Counselor; Present help; Comforter; Perfect Love; Trauma Remover; Chain Breaker; Purity; Innocence restorer; Guidance
Judgment	A negative force that causes heaviness
Mediator between God and man, the Man Christ Jesus	Just judge; the One who rules fairly on issues of our lives

SAY THIS AND NOT THAT

Christian Language	Words That Work
Need a doctor	Great Physician; physical and emotional healing
Old mindsets and lies people believe	Mind renewal; New way to think; God's way of thinking
Old things pass away, all things become new	Restored new start in the soul, mind, will, and emotions
Present help in time of trouble; Shield	Protector and Defender
Repentance	Turning your life completely around; leaving destructive lifestyles and now going the opposite direction into health
Restorer	Label removal, Label Remover; Removing false labels people put on us, even as children
Sin	Lifestyles and habits that separate us from Truth; A life change is necessary
Sinner	Seeker and friend of Jesus

WORDS THAT WORK

Christian Language	Words That Work
Sinner's prayer	No such thing in the Bible. However, you can speak prayers for them as they agree to accept the invitation for Jesus to live in their heart now too. Do this with open eyes, nothing religious.
Salvation	Organic restart; take your wrongdoings and wipe them from the record of your life, making you clean with a new start
The Way	Life director and spiritual compass with divine direction
Visionless; without a vision, people perish	Sight restorer, restoring vision and foresight for their lives
Who a person really is and what they are made for	Identity discovery
Wisdom	From the Ancient One, from above
Wisdom from above	Wisdom of Truth; secure direction, correction and certainty
Your name is now written in Lamb's book of life	God loves you, receives you, and writes your name in His book on the date you came to Him, and celebrates you.

ABOUT THE AUTHOR

Cindy McGill is a wife, mother, grandmother, and powerful servant of the Lord. It is almost impossible to describe her ministry in writing, as it is unique and diverse. She disciples believers and reaches out to those seeking God in the outer limits of society. Her passion is to help people find their life's purpose, receive healing from life trauma, and live their lives to the fullest by addressing the destructive issues we all face today.

Cindy travels internationally, teaching believers how to effectively engage the world we now live in. God has given her strategies on how to communicate Jesus to a world that doesn't know Him, His attributes, and His heart for them. She leads teams into some of the darkest, sin-filled places on earth to share the truth and love of Jesus. These extreme outreaches are to those the church has, by and large, turned away from including those in bondage to sexual addiction, sex trafficking, cutting, the occult, extreme addictions, alternative lifestyles, and more. Cindy is refreshingly real with no room for religious pretension.

The author of *What Your Dreams Are Telling You: Unlocking Solutions While You Sleep,* Cindy uses her gifts to help people understand how the Lord is speaking to them through dreams and what their dreams mean. She and her husband, Tim, have pastored for many years, and they now speak in conferences around the world and host boot camps to prepare teams for extreme outreaches and evangelism to this new generation of seekers.

Currently, Cindy and her husband, Tim, oversee the Encounter Service at OpenDoor Church in Burleson, Texas, every Saturday at 6 p.m. You can also connect with her through these channels:

Facebook: Facebook.com/cindymcgillofficial
Instagram: Instagram.com/cindy_mcgill_official
YouTube: YouTube.com/c/CindyMcGill
Website: CindyMcGill.org
Rumble: Rumble.com/c/c-519867

Made in the USA
Columbia, SC
09 August 2023